The Upside of Adversity might be best summed as an enriching story of how adversity became the platform for releasing God's real destiny in Os Hillman's life. Os's engaging, real-life description of the series of reversals he encountered as a successful Christian executive punctuate the times we have entered. The post-9/11 environment is demanding more—much more of those who are called by His name. As a pacesetter in God's emerging move in the marketplace, Os defines the steps for those called by God to make a difference in the business and professional areas of society.

MORRIS RUDDICK
PRESIDENT, GLOBAL INITIATIVES FOUNDATION
ENTREPRENEUR, CONSULTANT AND MINISTER
AUTHOR, *GOD'S ECONOMY, ISRAEL AND THE NATIONS*

Many people crash and burn when serious adversity comes their way. Others whine and say, "Life's unfair!" Os Hillman almost did both until God gave him the immensely practical revelation found in this book. Through it he discovered what he calls *The Upside of Adversity*, and you will discover the same amazing thing when you read this book!

C. PETER WAGNER
PRESIDING APOSTLE, INTERNATIONAL COALITION OF APOSTLES

Os Hillman has written a classic about Joseph, one of my favorite personalities of history. Joseph's ability to take adversity and turn it into strength is a lesson for all of us. Os weaves in his own story as well, and the end result is a book that will impact your life powerfully.

PAT WILLIAMS
AUTHOR AND SENIOR VICE PRESIDENT, ORLANDO MAGIC

Through the years of reading Os's work, I've sensed that he's growing in wisdom. That trajectory continues with *The Upside of Adversity*, a sensitive and clarifying look at a bewildering subject. Read it carefully, and it will help you.

MICHAEL ZIGARELLI
DEAN, REGENT UNIVERSITY SCHOOL OF BUSINESS

PRAISE FOR
THE UPSIDE OF ADVERSITY

The Upside of Adversity is the transparently honest journey of one who has failed yet come through that failure to see that God was at work during the entire process. Now, in God's timing, Os has become a key leader in the Faith at Work movement. I count it a privilege that he is both a colleague and friend. Regardless of your particular challenge, you will draw deeply from this book.

JOHN D. BECKETT
CHAIRMAN, THE BECKETT COMPANIES
AUTHOR, *MASTERING MONDAY: A GUIDE TO INTEGRATING FAITH AND WORK*

Understanding God's process for preparing and equipping his leaders to fulfill their work in this life is so valuable. Whether one is called to workplace leadership or pulpit ministry, the process of preparation is the same. This book will liberate and equip many to fulfill their calling.

DR. BILL HAMON
APOSTLE, BISHOP OF CHRISTIAN INTERNATIONAL MINISTRIES NETWORK (CIAN)
FOUNDER, CHRISTIAN INTERNATIONAL BUSINESS NETWORK (CIBN)
AUTHOR, *THE DAY OF THE SAINTS*

Are you facing a tough situation in your relationships, your workplace, your health or your finances? Os Hillman shares practical biblical insights and stories on how you can deal with the adversity and pass the test. I was personally helped by this book, and I strongly recommend it to any workplace leader.

KENT HUMPHREYS
PRESIDENT, FCCI / CHRIST@WORK

I never read a book by Os Hillman in which I have not been challenged by his God-given ability to find the hidden truths in Scripture. *The Upside of Adversity* will encourage you to see great truths from God's perspective in difficult times.

JOHNNY M. HUNT
PASTOR, FIRST BAPTIST CHURCH
WOODSTOCK, GEORGIA

It's sometimes difficult to see God at work in our lives. Anointed with wisdom and authority, Os Hillman shows how God uses adversity to bless us beyond our comprehension. *The Upside of Adversity* is a must-read for those going through challenging times.

LARRY JULIAN
AUTHOR, *GOD IS MY CEO AND GOD IS MY SUCCESS*

THE
UPSIDE
OF
ADVERSITY

OS HILLMAN

Regal

From Gospel Light
Ventura, California, U.S.A.

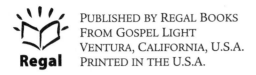

PUBLISHED BY REGAL BOOKS
FROM GOSPEL LIGHT
VENTURA, CALIFORNIA, U.S.A.
PRINTED IN THE U.S.A.

Library of Congress Cataloging-in-Publication Data
Hillman, Os.
  The upside of adversity / Os Hillman.
    p. cm.
  ISBN 0-8307-3916-5 (hardcover), 0-8307-4350-2 (trade paperback)
  1. Joseph (Son of Jacob) 2. Suffering—Biblical teaching. 3. Consolation. I. Title.
BS580.J6H55 2006
248.8'6—dc22   2006015989

1   2   3   4   5   6   7   8   9   10   /   10   09   08   07   06

Rights for publishing this book in other languages are contracted by Gospel Light Worldwide, the international nonprofit ministry of Gospel Light. Gospel Light Worldwide also provides publishing and technical assistance to international publishers dedicated to producing Sunday School and Vacation Bible School curricula and books in the languages of the world. For additional information, visit www.gospellightworldwide.org; write to Gospel Light Worldwide, P.O. Box 3875, Ventura, CA 93006; or send an e-mail to info@gospellightworldwide.org.

DEDICATION

To those who played a major part in helping me successfully walk through my adversity. May God bless your selfless service to me and the Lord.

Angie Hillman

Jim and Genie Mezick

Mike and Sue Dowgiewicz

J. Gunnar Olson

Although he was a son, he learned obedience
from what he suffered.

CONTENTS

ACKNOWLEDGMENTS

A good friend of mine is an executive editor and publisher for many well-known writers. One day as we were playing golf, I asked him about my new career as a writer. I told him that I've never really considered myself a good writer, but that I simply had something to say and decided to write it in a book. His comment was, "Os, there are authors and there are writers. An author has something to say that needs to be said, but they may need writers to help them say it. They only write on the subject they are passionate about. A writer, on the other hand, can write about any topic. He or she enjoys the technical skill of communicating through the written word."

"Ah!" I said. "I am an author! That makes sense."

I want to thank my friends at Regal Books: Bill Greig III, Kim Bangs, Roger Thompson and Steven Lawson, who decided this book was worthy of publication and helped craft it into the form you now see. Most importantly, I want to thank my wife, Angie, who edited the early manuscripts and gave me valuable feedback, and Jim Denney, who was my primary editor. Jim was an enormous asset who helped to shape the final manuscript into a cohesive and readable book.

Thank you, all!

FOREWORD

I never would have scheduled a block of time for a period of extraordinary pain and adversity in my life, but it happened anyway. On April 29, 2002, I was working with my son Ross, burning piles of brush and other debris at our new property in Woolsey, Georgia. After running out of diesel fuel to ignite the piles, I made the tragic decision to use gasoline.

I lit the match. In a split second, everything changed with a *whvoooom* of smoke and flames. I shouted, "Ross! Am I on fire?!" The sensations in my arms and face quickly became searing pain. I could not close my mouth because of the tightness of my skin. I could see melted skin hanging beneath my wrist.

During the first moments of pain and horror, I felt God's presence. From the LifeFlight helicopter ride to Grady Memorial Hospital in Atlanta to the painful daily hydrotherapy skin-removal treatments that followed, I had no doubt God was in charge and that this was part of the agenda He had for me.

Lying in the hospital bed, I had nothing but time—time to reflect, talk to people and experience the total peace of God's divine comfort. I realized that my schedule and God's divine calendar were not synchronized. His calendar always wins if there is a conflict.

God corrected my vision and enlarged my territory. I can now connect with people who have also passed through the flames of adversity. I experienced a new calling in my life—something that Os calls a "Joseph Calling."

Everyone has a natural tendency to sidestep obstacles, adversity or pain. We might be in the pit of extraordinary adversity or find ourselves there when God's calendar takes over. Os wrote *The Upside of Adversity* to help leaders use their experiences of adversity to expand their vision—to emerge with a deeper understanding of God and experience a richer relationship with Him and others. The only way to understand why God allows adversity is to interpret the events through a different perspective.

I encourage you to learn about Joseph and how the timeless principles of Scripture can apply to your life. God loves us so much that He uses our adversity experiences to teach, mold and polish our character—just as he did for Joseph.

Dan Cathy
CEO, Chick-fil-A

INTRODUCTION

Adversity.

We don't want to hear the word. We don't want to read about it or even think about it—until we find ourselves going through a painful trial. Then we are *forced* to think about it. Pain is a powerful motivator.

Because you are reading these words, chances are you are going through a time of adversity right now. No two experiences of adversity are exactly alike. One man loses a career and his dream dies. Another man watches his house burn to the ground. A couple walks away from the cemetery after burying a child. A woman receives a cancer diagnosis. Adversity comes in different shapes and sizes and degrees, but it all hurts. It *really* hurts.

I've been through adversity, and so have you. One thing I've learned is that God is always present in the midst of our suffering. He wants us to see adversity from His perspective so that we can live through it, learn from it, grow by it, and become the people He created us to be.

One of the central themes in this book is the Joseph Calling. In the book of Genesis, we meet a man named Joseph who experienced 13 years of adversity involving betrayal, mistreatment, enslavement, false accusation, imprisonment and separation from loved ones. But at the end of all of that suffering, when he was only 30 years old, Joseph was promoted to become the second-most influential leader on Earth. He became a spiritual and physical provider to his family, to a nation, and to the world.

That pattern—a prolonged but temporary experience of painful preparation, followed by a lifetime of leadership and ministry—is a common phenomenon. I've seen it in my own journey and in the lives of countless Christian leaders. After reading this book, you may discover that you are a modern-day Joseph.

These pages also chronicle a seven-year period of adversity that I experienced from 1994 to 2001. That experience allowed me to learn from others who have gone through adversity and have been transformed by it. In the process, I discovered that God has a great purpose for the problems and obstacles that we face in life. He uses adversity to prepare us for a lifetime of service to Him and to others.

The outcome of my trial of adversity was that God gave me an entirely new calling in life, a new sense of purpose, and a new direction that has taken me to more than 15 countries around the world. The Lord has written a more joyful ending to my story than I could have imagined. So I want to encourage you to trust God and persevere. Your suffering is not meaningless; it is a process of preparation. There is joy at the end of your trials. I pray that this book will encourage you and renew your hope as you prepare for the amazing future God has planned for you.

One final thought. As you read through each chapter, you will notice a key principle from each chapter is italicized to emphasize the lesson or application. I pray that this book will encourage you and renew your hope as you prepare for the amazing future that God has planned for you.

—Os Hillman

PART I

SOME LEADERS ARE CALLED TO EXTRAORDINARY ADVERSITY

You Have a Joseph Calling

*So it came about, when Joseph reached his brothers, that they
stripped Joseph of his tunic, the varicolored tunic that was on him;
and they took him and threw him into the pit.*

GENESIS 37:23-24, NASB

A man in a dark suit ushered me into the luxurious sitting room of the
penthouse suite. The windows of the room afforded a panoramic view
of the buildings and monuments of Washington, D.C. "He'll be with
you in a few moments," the man told me. Then he left me alone with
my thoughts.

"Lord," I prayed silently, "I've come more than 600 miles from
Atlanta to spend just a few minutes with the man I'm about to meet.
I hardly know anything about him. I made this appointment on the
basis of hearing an audiotape of a speech he gave. But, Lord, I know You
placed that tape in my hands for a purpose. Whatever you want me to
learn from this man, please open my ears and enable me to hear it."

A few minutes later, two men entered. One was tall and stately, with
an accent that seemed neither American nor purely European. The other
man was somewhat heavy-set and spoke with a Swedish accent. His
smile was warm and genuine. He put out his hand to take mine. "Hello,"
he said, "I'm Gunnar Olson."

I recognized his voice from the tape. J. Gunnar Olson—founder and president of the International Christian Chamber of Commerce (ICCC)—was a busy man. He was making final preparations for an international conference of the ICCC that very night. Even so, his manner was relaxed and unhurried. He introduced the other man, James Lockett, a member of the ICCC board.

The three of us sat down. It was late afternoon, and through the windows of the suite I could see that the skies over Washington were deepening toward evening.

"Tell me about yourself, Os," Gunnar said.

I briefly sketched my story. For 20 years, I had been a highly successful advertising executive. My list of clients read like a *Who's Who* of the corporate world: American Express, Steinway Pianos, Parisian Department Stores, ADP Payroll Services, Peachtree Software, and on and on. I was active in my church, and I led a men's Bible study. People thought I was the model Christian businessman.

But something had happened to change all of that. Two years earlier, beginning in the spring of 1994, I had experienced a series of catastrophic personal and business setbacks that destroyed my marriage and left me financially ruined. The past two years had left me feeling defeated as a Christian.

"To be candid, Mr. Olson," I concluded, "I'm not even sure why the Lord has led me here today. I don't know how you can help me. I only know that I feel like a complete failure. I've failed as a businessman, as a husband, as a father, and as a Christian. I know this sounds terrible to say, but it's true: I feel that God has abandoned me." With that, I fell silent.

Gunnar Olson and James Lockett looked at each other—and *laughed*!

I was prepared for just about any reaction to my story, but this response took me completely off guard. I had poured out all the pain of my shattered life before them—and they found it amusing?

My shock must have shown on my face, because Gunnar quickly turned to me and said, "Os, please don't be offended. We're not laughing at your pain but at the amazing way God works. James and I are simply astounded that the Lord keeps bringing people to us who have stories like yours! I tell you, Os, it's uncanny!"

"You mean, you know of other people who have gone through an experience like mine?" I said. "I've been feeling as if I were the only one!"

"Oh, you're hardly alone, my friend," Gunnar said. "In fact, your story fits a pattern so common that I have a name for it: the Joseph Calling. Os, you're not a failure. God has placed a Joseph Calling upon your life."

"What's a Joseph Calling?"

"Put simply, this is what it means: *Like Joseph, God calls some leaders to experience extraordinary levels of adversity in order to accomplish extraordinary things through them.* Why? Because He knows that adversity builds character and produces wisdom in the life of a leader. God will use this adversity for good in your life and in the lives of others. That's the principle of the Joseph Calling."

Gunnar then reminded me of the Old Testament story of Joseph, an innocent man who suffered misfortune and mistreatment, betrayal and false imprisonment. Yet it was those very experiences of adversity that prepared him to become one of the greatest leaders of the ancient world. I knew the story well—but it had never occurred to me to apply the lessons of Joseph's life to my own trials.

The moment I saw my adversity through the lens of the Joseph Calling, my perspective changed completely. I stopped seeing myself as a failure, abandoned by God. I realized that God had been dealing with me the same way He had dealt with Joseph. My losses, setbacks and trials had all been allowed—and even orchestrated—by a wise and loving God. Yes, Satan was also to blame for my failed marriage, because God is never behind marriages failing. Even so, God was preparing me for a larger role in leadership than I could ever imagine.

My first encounter with Gunnar Olson and the Joseph Calling took place in July 1996. Since then, I have discovered that everything Gunnar told me was true: There are thousands of Christians today who have the Joseph Calling upon their lives. They are entering, enduring or emerging from a time of terrible adversity—and God is preparing them for the challenge of godly leadership.

Joseph: A Leader Called to Adversity

When Joseph was born, his father, Jacob, was about 90 years old. Joseph was raised in the land of Canaan. As a teenager, Joseph tended Jacob's flocks of sheep.

There was terrible sibling rivalry among Jacob's 12 sons, 10 of whom were Joseph's half-brothers. Genesis 37:3 tells us that Jacob loved Joseph more than any of his other sons, because Joseph was born in Jacob's old age. In fact, Jacob gave Joseph an elaborately embroidered robe. This symbol of Jacob's favoritism made the brothers hate Joseph all the more.

On one occasion, Joseph had two dreams. In the first dream, Joseph and his brothers were binding sheaves of grain when suddenly Joseph's sheaf stood upright and the other sheaves bowed down to it. In the second dream, the sun, the moon and 11 stars all bowed down to Joseph. The dreams implied that Joseph would become a great leader who would have authority over his brothers.

When Joseph told these dreams to his brothers, they hated him even more. (Leaders are dreamers who look into the future and see reality before it comes to pass. Visionary dreamers often provoke jealousy in the people around them.) One day, when Joseph's jealous brothers saw him approaching their camp, they plotted to kill him. They said, "Here comes that dreamer! Let's kill him and see if his dreams still come true!" They seized him, stripped him of his robe and threw him into a pit. At that moment, Joseph discovered the meaning of the word "adversity."

As Joseph's brothers were sitting beside the pit and eating their meal, a Midianite trading caravan came by, heading for Egypt. One of Joseph's brothers, Judah, said, "I have an idea! Instead of killing Joseph, let's sell him to the slave merchants and make some money!" So they sold Joseph for 20 pieces of silver, and he was taken away to Egypt.

The slave traders sold Joseph to Potiphar, an official of the Pharaoh (king) of Egypt. The Lord gave Joseph success in Potiphar's employ, and Potiphar placed Joseph in charge of his staff of servants.

During this same time, however, Potiphar's wife noticed Joseph and repeatedly tried to seduce him. Joseph, being a godly young man of integrity, said, "My master—your husband—has entrusted me with his entire household. How could I betray that trust and sin against God by going to bed with you?"

Enraged by Joseph's rejection, Potiphar's wife accused him of raping her, telling her husband, "This is how your slave Joseph has treated me!" So Potiphar seized Joseph and put him in prison. Falsely accused and falsely imprisoned, Joseph found himself up to his neck in adversity.

While in prison, Joseph did a favor for one of his cellmates by interpreting a dream for him. That cellmate was the cupbearer of the Pharaoh. The cupbearer promised that if he got out of prison, he would do what he could to help Joseph. A few days later, the cupbearer was released. However, instead of keeping his promise, he forgot all about Joseph.

Two years passed while Joseph languished in prison, forgotten by the cupbearer. Two whole years! But God had not forgotten Joseph. He was preparing him for what was to come.

While Joseph was in prison, Pharaoh had a pair of disturbing dreams. He awoke frightened and troubled, and he demanded that his wise men tell him the meaning of the dreams—but no one could interpret the dreams. At that point, Joseph's former cellmate, the cupbearer, remembered Joseph and told Pharaoh that his Hebrew cellmate had correctly interpreted his dream. Pharaoh ordered that Joseph be brought to him.

Before Joseph could meet with Pharaoh, he first had to be bathed, shaved and scrubbed. When he finally came before Pharaoh, he was able to interpret the king's dreams: The land of Egypt would experience seven prosperous years followed by seven years of famine. If the nation would store up some of its abundance in the seven years of plenty, then the seven years of famine would not be so severe.

Pharaoh was so impressed by Joseph's wisdom that he made the 30-year-old Hebrew the second-most powerful leader in all of Egypt. Only Pharaoh himself had greater authority. Pharaoh put his own signet ring on Joseph's finger, dressed him in new robes, and placed a chain of gold around his neck. From then on, Joseph rode in Pharaoh's own chariot.

In the end, the dreams that Joseph dreamed back in the land of Canaan were fulfilled in the land of Egypt. Joseph did, indeed, become a great leader—and he eventually exercised authority over his own brothers. *But Joseph's dreams had to die before they could come true.* Joseph had to pass through betrayal, mistreatment, false accusation and false imprisonment before those dreams could be fulfilled.

That's what the Joseph Calling is all about. We dream a grand dream—and then the dream seems to wither and die in the face of adversity. We go through trials because adversity prepares us for leadership. Finally, when we have absorbed the lessons of adversity, God gives our dreams back to us and places us in a leadership position. Once there, God can use us in a way that He never could have if we had not passed through the pit of adversity. Ultimately, like Joseph, we become a spiritual and physical provider to those we are called to serve.

Why We Are Called to Adversity

When Gunnar Olson first explained the Joseph Calling to me, it was as if the scales fell from my eyes. I saw my life from a completely different perspective. I no longer viewed myself as a failure, rejected by God. I realized that God was still at work in my life, just as He was at work in Joseph's life throughout his trials. Once I realized that God had placed a Joseph Calling upon my life, all of my trials and losses began to make sense.

Adversity builds strength. Consider the butterfly. It begins life as a caterpillar, a wormlike larva that spins a cocoon for itself. For weeks, the larva remains hidden within the cocoon as it undergoes metamorphosis. When it's time for the butterfly to emerge, it must struggle and fight its way out of the cocoon. Watching this struggle, we might be tempted to help by tearing open the cocoon—but that's the worst thing we could do. A butterfly that is not allowed to struggle will emerge in a weakened state, unable to fly. Butterflies need adversity to become what God intended them to be. So do we.

The book of Job is probably the oldest book of the Bible, written even before Genesis. It's the story of a wealthy and successful community leader named Job. He was the Bill Gates or Donald Trump of his day—a fabulously successful businessman with huge holdings of livestock and real estate. He was also a deeply righteous and devoted follower of God.

Job 1 tells us that one day Satan came before God and God asked him, "Where have you come from?" Satan replied, "From roaming through the earth and going back and forth in it." In other words, Satan had been wandering the earth, trying to stir up trouble, misery and sin among human beings.

God said to Satan, "Have you considered my servant Job? There is no one on Earth like him; he is blameless and upright, a man who fears God and shuns evil." Notice that *God pointed Job out* to Satan! God practically painted a bull's-eye on Job's chest!

Satan said, "Does Job fear God for nothing? Have You not put a hedge around him and his household and everything he has? You have blessed the work of his hands so that his flocks and herds are spread throughout the land. But stretch out Your hand and strike everything he has, and he will surely curse You to Your face."

And the Lord replied, "Very well, then, everything he has is in your hands, but on the man himself do not lay a finger."

So Satan went out and proceeded to put poor Job through a trial of adversity. Job's herds were stolen, his servants were murdered, and all of Job's children were killed by a sudden tornado. On hearing the news, Job tore his robe, shaved his head and fell on his face before God, saying:

Naked I came from my mother's womb,
    and naked I will depart.
The LORD gave and the LORD has taken away;
    may the name of the LORD be praised (Job 1:21).

God didn't directly cause Job's losses. God didn't personally destroy Job's herds or kill Job's children. But God did point Job out to Satan, and He did give Satan permission to bring these losses into Job's life. In the process, Job underwent a kind of Joseph Calling experience. Through his trial of adversity, he grew in strength, wisdom and faith. His entire perspective on God was transformed by his suffering.

We must get beyond the immature notion that God is only interested in making us healthy, wealthy and happy. God wants so much more for us than that. He wants us to be wise, mature, obedient, bold and committed. He wants us to be like Christ. And the road to becoming like Christ often leads through the wilderness of adversity.

My Own Joseph Journey

I founded my own advertising agency in 1984. The next 10 years were boom years for my company, and I nearly became financially independent by the age of 42. Throughout these years of success, my Christian faith was important to me. I operated my company as a Christian witness, and I maintained a high standard of integrity. Our company was named The Aslan Group, after the lion Aslan, the Christlike-figure in C. S. Lewis's *Chronicles of Narnia*.

At the same time, I was experiencing deep problems in my marriage. Although my then-wife and I told few people about our problems, we were in counseling throughout our married life. We visited a number of counselors, seeking a solution to our problems. Finally, in March 1994, my wife decided that it was time to separate. After three and a half years of separation, the marriage ended in divorce. My only daughter was now a teenager.

We had just bought a 13-acre estate and were drawing up plans for our dream home. It was an idyllic setting, complete with a peaceful, meandering stream and a pasture for our horses. The house would sit on a hilltop. Just down the hill from the site of the house, we constructed a four-horse barn with an apartment upstairs. We planned to live in that apartment while the house was being built.

It was just after the barn and apartment were completed that my then-wife gave me the news that she wanted a separation—and that she and my daughter were moving into the apartment in the barn. I was devastated. I knew that we had serious problems, but I figured we'd eventually have a breakthrough in counseling and everything would be okay. Being a strong Christian, the word "divorce" was not in my vocabulary. Somehow, I reasoned, I'd find a way to change her mind.

Soon after the separation, I faced a series of ruinous crises in my business and financial life. First, our biggest client—one that represented 70 percent of our billings—decided to end our seven-year business relationship and fire us. To make matters worse, the client disputed a major campaign that we had just completed and refused to pay the bill—a little matter of $140,000!

Second, less than a month later, I noticed that I had stopped receiving financial reports from an investment company in which I had about $100,000 invested, both personal and business funds. It turned out that the company had gone out of business amid a flurry of lawsuits. Our money was gone—embezzled by one of the principals.

Third, a few weeks later, another investment company went under. This time, I lost about $200,000 of my own money, plus a sizable sum that my widowed mother had invested on my advice. The guilt I felt over the loss she suffered was unbearable.

The fourth business calamity I suffered was especially painful because it involved a trusted Christian brother. He was the vice president of my advertising company, the man who managed our second-largest account. I had confided in him and prayed with him during tough times. Then one day, he came to me and said, "Os, I'm leaving to form my own advertising company." It was a shock—but an even greater shock awaited me. A few days later, I learned that he had taken our second-largest account with him in violation of the non-compete agreement he had signed with me.

All of these personal and business calamities had befallen me within a space of a few months. Only a short time earlier, I had dreams, goals and forward momentum in my life. Now my dreams and my self-image lay shattered at my feet. I wondered why God had forsaken me. I couldn't go a single day without breaking down and crying. Sometimes, while talking to a friend, I would choke up in mid-sentence and start to weep.

During the first year following the breakup of my marriage, I felt as if I were paddling a rowboat with 10 holes in it while trying to bail out the water. As I tried to keep my company from bleeding to death, I struggled to maintain a relationship with my 12-year-old daughter, who was hurting even worse than I was. There was a period of about three weeks where I seemed to lose my relationship with her completely, because her view of me was tainted by the influence of my estranged wife. For a while, I wondered if my relationship with my daughter would ever be restored.

My pain was so great that I questioned the existence of God. Paradoxically, I was also angry with this God whose existence I doubted. The more that went wrong with my life, the angrier I became. I blamed my wife, the investment companies and my former business partner for these calamities and tragedies. I also blamed God.

I have learned that I have the kind of personality that demands to be in control. A controlling personality is usually driven by two forces: fear and pride. I lived with the fear that if I didn't control every situation, I would lose control of my life. I hesitated to delegate important tasks and decisions to others because I feared that other people wouldn't do things as well as I did. Most of all, I feared allowing God to have full control of my life. I realize now that my fear-based addiction to control was corrosive to my marriage.

I also had a problem with pride-based control. I had to maintain a good public image—the image of a successful, competent businessman with a strong Christian family. I couldn't let anyone know that I was flawed or that I lacked competence in any area. I couldn't bear the thought of people knowing that my marriage and my business were failing.

I tried desperately to reconcile with my wife, but she wouldn't budge. I tried desperately to recover my lost investments, but that was a lost cause. I tried desperately to save my advertising agency from ruin—I cut the agency staff from 10 people down to one (me), but I still lost money. My life was tumbling out of control. For a control addict, there is no worse fate than that!

I had lost everything that meant anything to me—my marriage, my relationship with my daughter, my business, my wealth, my self-esteem, my dreams and my faith in God. What did I have left to live for? I even considered having a car accident so that my family could collect on my $500,000 life insurance policy.

My trial of adversity, which I call my "Joseph Pit" experience, began in March 1994 and lasted until March 2001—exactly seven years, just like the seven years of famine in Egypt. During my trial, God sent a number of people to walk alongside me and help me understand what God was doing in my life. At the end of those seven years, God restored me in all aspects of my life—and He gave me a whole new reason for living.

Your Own Joseph Journey

I have written this book because there are thousands of people going through a journey like mine. I have written this book because I know how it feels to suffer adversity and feel abandoned by God. You may be in the Pit right now, but realize that God is at work in your life, using your adversity to prepare you for an amazing future.

Over the years, I've found that very few people understand the Joseph Calling. Pastors don't. Business leaders don't. Well-meaning family members don't. I didn't begin to understand it myself until I walked into that Washington, D.C., penthouse and Gunnar explained it to me.

Now I take this message wherever I go. I share these truths through my speaking and workshops. Every time I talk about the Joseph Calling, people come to me and say, "I've never heard this before! I've felt completely alone with my pain! I thought God had turned His back on me!"

God used Gunnar Olson as a lifeline when I needed one. Now I'm privileged to see God using me as a lifeline of hope to others. I could never have had this ministry if I had not gone through the pit of adversity. Today, I'm grateful for what I've learned through that experience of pain and loss. What looked like a pit of despair at the time became a launching pad for the ministry I have today.

What does your Pit look like? How deep is it? How wide? How dark? How painful? No two Joseph Pit experiences are alike. Yours may entail the loss of a career, financial setbacks, a crisis in your marriage, the loss of loved ones, the loss of your health, or any of a thousand other trials or calamities.

But one thing is consistent in every Joseph Pit experience: Our life is interrupted. We lose control over our circumstances. We are cast upon a sea of uncertainty with a raft but no oars. For the first time in our life, we are forced to depend entirely on God and others.

If that is how you feel right now, I want to give you hope for your future. God has selected you to embark on the journey of a lifetime.

He has chosen you to join the select company of people like Job and Joseph, Daniel and Paul—people who have undergone adversity and emerged as people of refined character and enlarged leadership ability. I want to give you the same message that God imparted to me through Gunnar Olson: *You have a Joseph Calling upon your life.* In this time of adversity, God is preparing you. He's getting ready to use you in a mighty way. And He will turn your Valley of Achor (Trouble) into a door of hope.

QUESTIONS FOR REFLECTION

1. How do you normally respond when you find yourself in a crisis of adversity? How would you like to respond?

2. What parallels do you see between the journey of Joseph and your own journey in life? What lessons or encouragement can you draw from those parallels?

3. What are your feelings as you reflect on the adversity that you are experiencing right now? Are you angry about the situation that you are in? With whom are you angry? God? Yourself? Your spouse? Other family members? People in your church? People in your business circles? Others?

4. What is the prayer of your heart right now? How would you like other people to be praying for you? Have you asked a trusted Christian friend to be your partner in praying for that need in your life?

2

GOD'S WAY OF
CALLING A LEADER

*The Spirit of the LORD will come upon you in power, and you will prophesy
with them; and you will be changed into a different person.*

1 SAMUEL 10:6

When Gunnar Olson invited me to an international gathering of Christian
workplace leaders on the island of Cyprus, I could only laugh. It was 1998,
and I was four years into my Joseph Pit experience. I couldn't afford taxi
fare, much less a flight to Cyprus. I wasn't even sure where Cyprus was.
I had to check a map to learn that it's in the eastern Mediterranean Sea,
south of Turkey. A trip to Cyprus was out of the question.

The next day, I received a call from a man I'd met a couple of months
earlier. "What are you doing tomorrow?" he said.

"Just working at the office," I replied.

"How about riding to the airport with me? I want to talk with you
about a project I'd like you to participate in."

I agreed, and the next day we drove to the airport together.

"We're going to pick up a friend of mine," he said as we drove. "He's
a missionary in Cyprus. He's helping to host a conference there in March
with Gunnar Olson. Had you heard of the conference?"

Amazed, I told him that Gunnar had invited me to attend that very
event.

"Oh, you really should go! We're planning to take some business-people to this conference. I wanted to ask you to come give your 'Called to the Workplace' workshop to these men on the trip. We'll pay your expenses plus an honorarium. What do you say?"

To say that I was shocked would be the understatement of the millennium! I was on my way to Cyprus! Again, I had to laugh. I was sure that God was orchestrating events in a miraculous manner to assure me of His presence.

Or was He? A few weeks before I was to finalize my travel arrangements, I received word that this man hadn't been able to sign up any other businesspeople for the trip. My trip was canceled. I thought, *Well, I guess it wasn't God's will for me to go after all.*

A short time later, my friend Clark told me about a $1,500 scholarship that would enable me to go to Cyprus as a representative of his church—which was all the more amazing because I wasn't even a member of his church! So, in March 1998, I attended the ministry conference in Cyprus.

During the conference, a man approached me and said, "The Lord wants you to know that He had to remove your finances in order for you to receive the reward He has for you in heaven. He says, 'You've remained close to Me because of your dependence on Me during these times.'" I had never met this man before, and he knew nothing about me. He was from England; I was from the United States. Yet God had given him a message I needed to hear—and the words he spoke made perfect sense in light of what I had experienced during the preceding four years.

This man and I talked for a while, and our hearts bonded as he told me of his own journey through adversity. He told me how he had once spent time in prison for a crime he didn't commit, and that God had used that experience to draw him closer to the Lord. We concluded our visit with prayer. As we prayed, the man stopped and looked at me with astonishment. "I have a picture in my mind," he said. "I see a large orange tree with much fruit on it—fruit that is now beginning to ripen and fall from the tree. You are that tree! You are about to bear much fruit."

That was a startling statement for two reasons. First, during the conference in Cyprus, we were served large, juicy oranges with our buffet dinners. I enjoyed these oranges so much that I always took a few back to my room for an evening snack. When my friend from England told me that I was like an *orange* tree that was about to bear *much fruit*, I immediately thought of the sweetness of those oranges.

Second, this image was startling because during the first few years of my Joseph Pit experience, two other people had made similar statements. The first occasion was in June 1995, less than a year after my separation from my wife. I was on a business trip to Seattle and attended church one evening with friends. During the worship time, three people prayed over me, and one of them described a picture he saw: "I see a series of trees with fruit on them. The first row was small. Over your life, you have eaten from row upon row of trees, each row larger than the one before. You have been eating of this fruit over your lifetime. You have not eaten from one larger tree. After you do, your relationship with God will never be the same." (The larger tree he spoke of was the tree of betrayal, which I would experience later.)

The second occasion was 21 months later, in February 1997, the night before the first Marketplace Leaders Summit in Atlanta. A Christian brother told me, "I see a tree that has been replanted into new soil. You are the tree." Now, for a third time, someone had described my life as a tree—and for the first time, I was being told that I was about to bear much fruit. God was using different people in different parts of the world to reveal a progressive vision of His activity in my life. Clearly, the Lord was trying to get a message of hope and encouragement to me.

When the man described this image of the tree bearing fruit, I wept. I was overwhelmed by the fact that God cared so much for me that He would send this series of images of my life—symbolic images that assured me that He was making my life fruitful even in the midst of my adversity. At that moment, I felt that I knew how Joseph must have felt when God enabled him to interpret dreams while he was undergoing adversity in an Egyptian prison.

Adversity: God's Pathway to Leadership

From my experience and study of the Scriptures, I've observed this principle: *The pathway to leadership almost always takes us through the valley of adversity.* We see this principle not only in the story of Joseph but also in the lives of many other leaders in both the Old and New Testaments.

Moses was raised in the royal splendor of Pharaoh's household in Egypt, but he was forced to flee and spend 40 years in desert exile before God spoke from a burning bush and called him to lead the Hebrew people. Joshua spent the years of his youth as a slave in Egypt and his middle-aged years wandering in the desert at Moses' side. He was well acquainted with adversity when God called him to lead Israel's armies in the conquest of Canaan. The prophet Daniel had to pass through a fiery furnace and a den of hungry lions before he could reach a place of power and influence in the Babylonian courts. And we see this same pattern played out in the lives of David, Isaiah, Amos, Hosea and other Old Testament leaders.

Turning to the New Testament, we see that even Jesus had to face adversity in the desert, suffering hunger, thirst, temptation and opposition from Satan. Only then could He begin His public ministry. The Lord's disciples had to endure the loss of their Master, the failure of their own faith and character, and the dark days of despair between the cross and the empty tomb before they could become the founding leaders of the Lord's church.

And then there was the apostle Paul, who was struck blind on the road to Damascus. Paul and adversity became lifelong friends. He was beaten with rods three times, stoned once, shipwrecked three times and nearly flogged to death five times. He was constantly in danger from bandits, corrupt religious authorities, the Roman oppressors and others. Yet despite this adversity, Paul concluded:

> We are hard pressed on every side, but not crushed; perplexed, but not in despair; persecuted, but not abandoned; struck down, but not destroyed. We always carry around in our body the death of Jesus, so that the life of Jesus may also be revealed in our body (2 Cor. 4:8-10).

It's hard to find anyone in Christian history who became a great leader without earning an advanced degree at the University of Adversity. John Bunyan (1628-1688), the author of *The Pilgrim's Progress*, grew up in poverty and taught himself to read. As a young man, he struggled with feelings of not being forgiven by God and was tortured by visions of eternal punishment. His devout wife helped him to overcome his fear, but then, while she was still in her twenties, she died of a sudden illness. In his grief, Bunyan devoted himself to preaching. The English government, however, repeatedly imprisoned him for preaching without a license.

On one occasion, Bunyan was sentenced to three months in prison, but when he told the officials he intended to go on preaching, his sentence was extended to 12 years. Like Joseph, John Bunyan experienced God's presence in a special way while he was in prison. In fact, it was in his cell that he penned his enduring classic, *The Pilgrim's Progress*. It's a book that could only have been written by a soul that was refined by the fires of adversity.

God is always in control, achieving His objectives through our lives. The psalmist described how this principle worked in the life of Joseph:

> [God] called down famine on the land
>> and destroyed all their supplies of food;
> and he sent a man before them—
>> Joseph, sold as a slave.
> They bruised his feet with shackles,
>> his neck was put in irons,
> till what he foretold came to pass,
>> till the word of the LORD proved him true.
> The king sent and released him,
>> the ruler of peoples set him free.
> He made him master of his household,
>> ruler over all he possessed,
> to instruct his princes as he pleased
>> and teach his elders wisdom (Ps. 105:16-22).

A. W. Tozer once wrote, "It is doubtful whether God can bless a man greatly until he has hurt him deeply." God has a mission for your life and for mine. But before we can carry out that mission, we must go through the boot camp of adversity.

Not a Detail Left to Chance

We see another example of how God used adversity for good in the Old Testament story of King Saul. In 1 Samuel 9 and 10, we find Saul working in the family business, employed by his father, Kish. The passage doesn't tell what type of business Kish had, but we know it involved donkeys. In Bible times, donkeys represented trade and commerce. They were the primary means of transporting goods.

Some of Kish's donkeys were missing, so Kish told his son Saul to take a servant with him to go and find them. Saul and the servant traveled the countryside searching for the missing donkeys, but without results. After several days, Saul thought his father might worry about him, so he told the servant, "Let's go back."

The servant replied, "Look, in this town there's a man of God, a prophet. Let's go see him and maybe he will tell us which way to take." In today's terminology, it was time to call in a consultant.

So Saul and the servant trudged up the hill to the city. As they went through the town, the prophet—a man named Samuel—walked toward them along the street. This was no accident. The previous day, God had told Samuel, "About this time tomorrow I will send a man to you. Anoint him as the leader over My people, the nation of Israel." As Samuel walked toward Saul, God told the prophet, "The man who is approaching is the one I told you about. He will be the leader of My people."

Saul stopped Samuel in the street and said, "Sir, would you please tell me how to find the house of the prophet?"

"I'm the prophet you're looking for," Samuel replied. "Today you'll have dinner with me, and tomorrow I'll tell you everything that is in your heart."

When Saul heard Samuel's prophecy, he thought the prophet was mistaken! He said, "I'm from the tribe of Benjamin, the smallest and least important of all the tribes of Israel. Our little tribe has never produced a king! How can you make such a statement?"

Saul felt incompetent and unworthy to lead the nation. However, in the end, Samuel anointed Saul with oil and made him king over all of Israel. Saul's pathway to leadership led through the experience of a business setback: a missing herd of donkeys. God arranged every step of Saul's journey.

It was God who sent the donkeys away, which made it necessary for Saul to go search for them. When Saul was ready to give up the search, God arranged for the servant to suggest that they look for a prophet in a nearby city. The Lord spoke to the prophet and told him to expect Saul's arrival. There was not a single detail left to chance. God's plan worked flawlessly.

So it is in your life and mine. God is in control. He has a plan for getting us to the destination He has appointed for us. We don't have to manipulate events, for God Himself is in control of all divine appointments. If you are going through a Joseph Pit experience right now, realize that God has a ministry planned for you that you can't even imagine. Just keep pressing into God with all your heart.

Hiding Under the Baggage

Let's take a closer look at Saul's response to God's calling. First Samuel 9:21 tells us that when Samuel told Saul that God had chosen him to be king, Saul answered, "But am I not a Benjamite, from the smallest tribe of Israel, and is not my clan the least of all the clans of the tribe of Benjamin? Why do you say such a thing to me?"

At first glance, this sounds like a humble response. It sounds as if Saul is blushing and digging his big toe in the dirt, saying, "Aw, shucks. I'm just a little ol' Benjamite. I'm not worthy to be a king."

But Saul is not responding in genuine humility. He's responding in *false* humility. True humility means being obedient and eager to serve God. Samuel himself, when God called him as a child, responded, "Speak, for your servant is listening" (1 Sam. 3:10). When God called Isaiah to deliver His message to the nation of Israel, Isaiah responded, "Here am I. Send me!" (Isa. 6:8). And when God called a young woman named Mary to be the mother of the Savior, she responded without hesitation, "I am the Lord's servant. May it be to me as you have said" (Luke 1:38).

Saul responded differently. He responded with denial and false humility. His response reveals both arrogance and a lack of authentic faith in God. Genuine faith means being ready to believe that God is able to accomplish even the unthinkable. But false humility says, "No, Lord. I'm busy living my life on my terms. I'm directing my own path, thank You very much. You're going to have to find someone else for the job."

When God begins to refine us and prepare us for leadership, one of the first things He has to do is *burn the self-centered pride out of us*. He has to turn us upside-down and shake us, humble us and level us. He doesn't need our skill, our talent, or our ability. He can find hundreds, thousands, millions of other people who are as skilled and talented as we are. He wants our hearts to be yielded to Him.

When the day came for Saul to be crowned king of Israel, he was nowhere to be found. Why? Because he had second thoughts about God's plan for his life—so he hid! He was focused on his own limitations, not the limitless power of God. So the Lord told Samuel, "[Saul] has hidden himself among the baggage" (1 Sam. 10:22).

You and I are a lot like Saul, are we not? We focus on our weakness instead of on God's strength. We hide ourselves among the baggage— the emotional baggage of guilt and regret, of past failures and sins, of old wounds and emotional hurts. Instead of embracing God's calling, we run and hide beneath the baggage of the past.

I recall the first time people associated my name with being a leader in the Faith at Work movement. I was just as surprised as anyone—even though God had told me during a three-day fast in 1996 that He was going to do this through me. I was an unlikely candidate for such a calling. I was deep in debt, facing divorce and suffering financial calamity. *But God is more concerned with future potential than present circumstances.*

The scene of Saul hiding among the baggage is comical. Saul is described as standing a head taller than every other man in Israel—yet he hid and tried to make himself invisible.

But are we any less absurd? We are children of the King, servants of the Creator of the Universe—but when He calls us, we hide. We say, "Who am I? A nobody! I don't have any leadership ability. I'm in debt. I'm divorced. I'm in a dead-end job. I have no degrees, no impressive résumé. Just let me hide." *God often takes us through adversity to get our eyes off of our own limitations so that we can see His limitless power.*

Becoming a Different Person

Henry Blackaby, author of *Experiencing God*, once wrote, "You cannot go with God and stay where you are." Whenever God moves us in a new direction, we have to change. Yes, change takes us out of our comfort zone—but nothing of value was ever accomplished in a comfort zone! To become the people God wants us to be, we must allow Him to reshape us and make us new. We see this truth in the life of Saul.

After Samuel anointed Saul, he prophesied to Saul, saying, "The Spirit of the LORD will come upon you in power, and you will prophesy with them; and you will be changed into a different person" (1 Sam. 10:6). Imagine that! The Spirit of God changed Saul into a different person than he had been before! The old Saul had to pass away; the Saul who would be king had to become a new creation.

God wants to do no less in our lives. He wants to change us into different people—into new creations. He wants to reshape us so that we reflect the character of Jesus Christ. We can't accomplish God's plan for our lives by staying as we are. As Paul tells us:

> Do not conform any longer to the pattern of this world, but be transformed by the renewing of your mind. Then you will be able to test and approve what God's will is—his good, pleasing and perfect will (Rom. 12:2).

We can't demonstrate God's good and perfect will for our life by staying in the same old rut. We must be transformed and renewed. That's why we must often pass through adversity on our way to becoming what God wants us to be. Adversity changes us. Adversity is the crucible that melts down the *old us*. Adversity is the hammer that shapes the *new us*.

When God transforms us, He forms a new partnership—a team with a mission for achieving His purposes in the world. When Saul was crowned king of Israel, he did *not* become an absolute monarch. He became part of a team, a three-way partnership that also included the Lord God and the prophet Samuel. God was in control—but He exercised that control through the prophet and the king.

The same is true of our own lives. When we yield our lives to God, a new partnership is formed: God the Father, Jesus the Son, the Holy Spirit and us. We are not the monarchs of our own lives. We are team players, and we answer to God.

How God Confirms His Calling on Our Lives

How do we know that God is calling us to a new direction in our lives? We may *feel* that God is prodding us in a new direction, but how do we *know* that it's true? What if we are being swept away by emotion or wishful thinking? What if we are misreading God's will?

These are important questions. When something new happens in our lives, we need to know that it's really of God. Fortunately, God provides a way of confirming His calling on our lives. We catch a glimpse of God's method of confirming His will in the story of Saul:

> Then Samuel took a flask of oil and poured it on Saul's head and kissed him, saying, "Has not the LORD anointed you leader over his inheritance? When you leave me today, you will meet two men near Rachel's tomb, at Zelzah on the border of Benjamin. They will say to you, 'The donkeys you set out to look for have been found. And now your father has stopped thinking about them and is worried about you. He is asking, "What shall I do about my son?"'" (1 Sam. 10:1-2).

At this point, Saul had no proof that God had chosen him as king except for Samuel's word. Saul had to know if Samuel was truly from God—or if he was just a religious nut who had spent too much time under the desert sun.

So God provided Saul with evidence that gave him assurance and confirmation that Samuel truly spoke for God. God confirmed Samuel's word and Saul's calling by restoring something important to Saul that he had lost: the missing donkeys. God solved the very problem that Saul had tried to solve when he left home. Now Saul not only had his problem solved, but he also had a completely new purpose for his life.

Has God stirred up and shaken your world as He did Saul's? Have you been forced to make major changes in your life? Do you sense that God is placing a new calling on your life?

Then here is my counsel: *Be alert to the people God brings into your life during this crucial time.* Share your thoughts, your vision and your questions with people who demonstrate sensitivity to the Spirit's leading. Ask those people to pray for you. Listen for words of wisdom and confirmation. Ask God to help you hear and recognize His voice in the counsel you receive.

When God confirms His will to you, step out boldly! Let God use you in ways you never dreamed of before.

From the Land of Bondage to the Land of Promise

Becoming a new person is part of a journey that begins at conversion. Before coming to Christ, we were living (in a metaphorical sense) in Egypt, in the land of bondage. Just as the people of Israel toiled as slaves in Egypt, we were slaves to sin and worldly ambition. The apostle Paul put it this way:

> But thanks be to God that, though you used to be slaves to sin, you wholeheartedly obeyed the form of teaching to which you were entrusted. You have been set free from sin and have become slaves to righteousness (Rom. 6:17-18).

Before we came to Christ, we sweated and toiled to build our career and acquire material possessions. Work was our idol. Greed was our taskmaster. We may have had all the trappings of power in the business world—a corner office, a staff of our own, a key to the executive washroom—but we were living as a slave in the land of Egypt. We didn't run our career; our career ran us.

Jesus once said, "No servant can serve two masters. . . . You cannot serve both God and Money" (Luke 16:13). In the original language, the word translated "Money" was an Aramaic word, *Mammon*. This does not refer merely to money as a medium of exchange but also to a mind-set of ambition for riches, power and worldly gain. The word is capitalized in the original text because the people of Jesus' day thought of Mammon as a false god. Jesus was saying that those who spend their lives seeking worldly gain are idolaters. No one can serve two masters. No one can worship both the true God and a false god.

If we serve Mammon, we are living as a slave in Egypt. We cannot experience the grace that God gives to His children because we are too busy striving for riches and enslaved to our true master, Mammon. The only way we can be free is to turn away from Mammon and allow the one true God to transform us into a different person. Then we will no longer be slaves. We will have rest. As the psalmist writes:

> In vain you rise early
> > and stay up late,
> toiling for food to eat—
> > for he grants sleep to those he loves (Ps. 127:2).

When we asked Jesus to be our Savior and Lord, He began a process of reshaping us to make us more like Himself. He began stripping away all the things that didn't contribute to us becoming more like Christ. This is a painful process, involving varying degrees of adversity. In general, I've observed that *the greater and higher the calling, the more intense the adversity.*

One sign that we are becoming more like Christ is that we begin to lose our attachment to our own wants and interests. We stop expecting God to serve our needs and instead seek to serve His purposes. To put it bluntly, *we die to ourselves,* to our desires, to our ambitions, to our wants. We begin to seek His face, not just His hand in our lives, and our prayers become an incense of praise, adoration and submission to His will.

As we die to self and become totally yielded to God, we may sometimes experience greater material blessing and career success than we had before the crisis. But sometimes we may experience failure and loss. Romans 6:4 tells us that we are buried with Christ through baptism and that after death and burial comes resurrection—either in this life or in the life to come. Hebrews 11:39 tells us that while many believers do not receive the fulfillment of God's promise in this life, they will all receive the fulfillment of perfection in the life to come. So whether we experience restoration in this life or the next depends on God's ultimate purpose for our lives.

One of the signs that we are truly becoming different people is that our faith remains steady even when our circumstances change. If we are truly becoming more like Christ, we don't let changing circumstances throw us. We remain on an even keel regardless of success or failure, comfort or stress. Why? *Because we are dead to circumstances but alive in Christ.*

A dead man can't be anxious. A dead man can't be stressed. A dead man has no worries. That's why Paul tells us to "count yourselves dead to sin but alive to God in Christ Jesus" (Rom. 6:11). That's why Jesus said, "If anyone would come after me, he must deny himself and take up his cross daily and follow me. For whoever wants to save his life will lose it, but whoever loses his life for me will save it" (Luke 9:23-24). If we are living as slaves—in bondage to worldly desires and ambitions—there is only one way to freedom: *We have to die.*

When Moses led the people of Israel out of Egypt, he took them to the edge of the Red Sea. The people saw the sea before them and heard the chariots of the Egyptians behind them. They knew they were trapped—and they lost their faith in God. They thought God was no longer at work in their lives. In panic and despair, they turned on Moses and said, "Why did you bring us out into the desert to die? When we were slaves in Egypt, didn't we tell you, 'Just leave us alone and let us continue serving the Egyptians.' Better to live as slaves than to die out here!"

The people of Israel didn't understand that God had planned all along to bring them to that place of despair, trapped between Pharaoh and the sea. They couldn't imagine that God's path to freedom actually led straight into and *through* the deep waters!

The waters of the Red Sea, like the New Testament sacrament of baptism, are a symbol of death. When Moses stretched out his hand

and the Lord parted the Red Sea, the people of Israel walked upon the dry seabed with walls of water on either side. They descended into the depths of the sea, and then rose again. They died to their old selves and rose to a new life that led to the Promised Land.

You and I can identify with the people of Israel in their journey. During our trial of adversity, we panic and cry out to God, "Why did You bring me out into this desert of adversity to die?" We would rather live as slaves than die to self and yield control of our lives to God. But God knows where He is leading us. He is taking us through the depths so that we can emerge as new people, ready to enter the Promised Land.

Shedding Former Things

God is calling thousands of people out of Egypt, out of their old lives of bondage. He's calling them to become new people, living out His plan for their lives in the Promised Land, a land flowing with milk and honey. God wants Christians who are refined by adversity to take their places in the financial marketplace, the corridors of commerce, the capitals of information and entertainment, and the halls of government.

As we answer God's calling on our lives, we face the same challenges that the people of Israel faced as they made their way into the Promised Land. When the people of Israel crossed over the Jordan River and set foot upon the land of promise, God told Joshua to make flint knives and revive a ritual that had fallen into disuse: circumcision.

The rite of circumcision, of course, is the surgical removal of the foreskin (prepuce) of the penis. This rite was established as a sign of God's covenant with Abraham in Genesis 17, but it had not been practiced during the 40 years that Israel wandered in the wilderness before reaching the Promised Land. Joshua obeyed God's command and had all the Israelite men circumcised at a place they called Gibeath Haaraloth (a rather graphic name that means "hill of foreskins").

The rite of circumcision is bloody and painful, and the Israelite men were incapacitated until the wound healed. But after the men healed, God told Joshua, "Today I have rolled away the reproach of Egypt from you" (see Josh. 5:9). When Israel responded in obedience, God removed the shame of slavery from the nation.

With the removal of the foreskins, the men of Israel became a *new* and *different* people. They were no longer slaves of the past; they were free people with a future. It was time to put aside the old way of life and to put Egypt behind them. More important, it was time to enter the Promised Land with confidence and power.

Circumcision represents the shedding of former things. It also represents testing, obedience, pain and a humbling of the self before God. Once the former things have been removed, God pronounces His blessing: The reproach and shame of bondage are removed. Those who have been circumcised are ready to inhabit a land flowing with milk and honey.

Does this mean that all of our troubles are over? No. We should never forget that the real testing began once Israel crossed the Jordan and entered the Promised Land. Israel couldn't just walk in and set up housekeeping. There was a price to be paid—the price of war.

In fact, the people of Israel fought *39 major battles* before the Promised Land came under their control. The Israelites couldn't compromise with the evil and idolatry that were in the land. They had to cast them out. As Paul tells us, "our struggle is not against flesh and blood, but against the rulers, against the authorities, against the powers of this dark world and against the spiritual forces of evil in the heavenly realms" (Eph. 6:12-13). As believers, we will always be in a battle against evil until the war is won.

God does not force us to move into the Promised Land. Many Israelites refused to enter the Promised Land and died in the desert. We, too, are free to disobey and die in the desert if we so choose. We are free to reject the destiny that God offers us. But why waste the one and only irreplaceable life that He has given us? God has designed a bright future for us—and it's ours if we accept His calling and cling to Him as He reshapes us and remakes us in the wilderness of adversity.

Many years ago, an anonymous poet wrote these lines to describe how God shapes us and refines us for His use:

When God wants to drill a man,
And thrill a man,
And skill a man;
When God wants to mold a man
To play the noblest part,
When He yearns with all His heart
To create so great and bold a man
That all the world shall be amazed,
Watch His methods, watch His ways—
How He ruthlessly perfects
Whom He royally elects.
How He hammers him and hurts him,
And with mighty blows, converts him
Into trial shapes of clay
Which only God understands,
While his tortured heart is crying,
And he lifts beseeching hands.
How He bends but never breaks
When his good He undertakes.
How He uses whom He chooses,
And with every purpose, fuses him,
By every act, induces him
To try His splendor out.
God knows what He's about.

QUESTIONS FOR REFLECTION

1. Are you living in the land of Egypt or in the Promised Land? Use the following checklist to evaluate where you are in your journey:

LAND OF EGYPT

__ I live by sweat and toil. I feel trapped by my lifestyle and my career.

__ I view myself as a slave.

__ I feel forced to work, a slave to Mammon.

__ I know about Jesus (intellectual knowledge).

__ My relationship with God is activity-based. I work hard to make myself acceptable to God.

__ My heart is uncircumcised. I live for myself and my worldly ambition.

__ I sense that I have a rebellious heart. I don't want to yield control of my life, my plan or my future to God.

__ I feel what's mine is mine. I earned it; I own it.

__ I am independent. I make my own decisions.

THE PROMISED LAND

__ I live by obedience, trusting in God's provision.

__ I view myself as an heir of the King.

__ I am free to work as part of my worship to God.

__ Jesus is my personal friend (genuine relationship).

__ My relationship with God is based on my love and gratitude to Him.

__ My heart is circumcised. I am a new person; I live for God's kingdom.

__ I have a new, willing, yielded heart. I have trusted God with full control of my life, and I want to serve His purposes.

__ I believe that everything I have comes from God. He owns it; I merely manage it.

__ I am on God's team. I make cooperative decisions under His authority.

Continued on next page

LAND OF EGYPT

__ I live for my own goals and pleasures.

__ I feel at peace with the world and at odds with God.

__ I use debt to finance my wants and my status symbols. I am a slave to debt.

__ I obey only out of fear of punishment.

__ I live by rules and fear of being rejected by God (legalism).

THE PROMISED LAND

__ I live for a cause greater than myself.

__ I feel at peace with God and in conflict with the world.

__ I avoid debt and live within my means. I tithe and give sacrificially to God.

__ I obey because I listen and follow the Shepherd's voice.

__ I live joyfully by trusting in God's love (grace).

If this checklist reveals that you are still living in Egypt instead of the Promised Land, why not stop right now, talk to God, and yield your life at this very moment to His plans and purposes for your life?

2. What was God's ultimate goal for Joseph? For Saul? For the nation of Israel?

3. What is God's ultimate goal for you as you go through your Joseph Pit experience?

THE BLACK HOLE

My grace is sufficient for you, for my power is made perfect in weakness.

2 CORINTHIANS 12:9

On February 20, 1962, at 9:47 A.M., the spacecraft *Friendship 7* rose on a pillar of fire, piloted by lone astronaut John Glenn. Leaving the coast of Florida far behind, the space capsule orbited the earth three times, traveling 81,000 miles in less than four hours. As the craft began its descent from space, mission controllers in Houston received a warning signal: A sensor indicated that the capsule's heat shield was in danger of detaching. If the heat shield came loose during re-entry, the capsule would burn like a meteor—and John Glenn would die.

There was no way to fix the problem in space. The capsule was already approaching the outer fringe of the atmosphere. As the tiny spacecraft fell toward Earth, the heat shield glowed red-hot—then white-hot. Soon, a hot cloud of ionized gas particles called *plasma* surrounded the capsule. Because radio waves cannot penetrate plasma, the spacecraft experienced a total communications blackout—what astronauts and mission controllers call a "black hole" (not to be confused with the black holes that form in space when a star collapses).

The minutes crawled by and the suspense mounted in the Houston control room. NASA engineers felt totally helpless. Finally, after five minutes of silence, mission controllers heard Glenn's voice crackling over the radio: *"Friendship 7* to Houston—"

Shouts of joy shook the control room. John Glenn was coming home.

It turned out that the warning signal had come from a faulty sensor. Although neither Glenn nor the mission controllers knew it at the time, the heat shield was absolutely firm and reliable. The fears for John Glenn's safety during his black-hole experience were unfounded.

If you've ever been through a Joseph Pit experience, you probably know what a communications "black hole" feels like. While you are in the pit of adversity, you feel that your world is collapsing, that your life is out of control—and that God is silent. You call out to Him and there is no answer. The silence of a black-hole is deafening. You feel isolated and alone. You question God's love, His care for you, and even His existence.

But even when it seems that God is distant and silent, when you feel you are in a black hole of isolation and loneliness, your "heat shield" is still there, firm and reliable. In your black-hole experience, God is teaching you to go deeper into your relationship with Him. You may think that your life is out of control and burning like a meteor, but in reality God, your heat shield, still protects you from the fiery forces that surround you.

I discovered this truth during my own black hole, a two-year period from 1994 to 1996, the first two years of my seven-year Joseph Pit trial. The black hole usually occurs at the front end of a crisis when the heat is greatest—and when God seems strangely silent.

A Place of Total Nothingness

A black hole is a place of total nothingness. It's a time in our life when God removes the resources and supports that we normally rely on to feel secure—our careers, finances, friends, family, health, and so forth. For years, we may have thought that we were trusting in God, but in reality, we were trusting in people and things for our own sense of safety. Suddenly, everything we have relied on vanishes—and we feel naked and defenseless against the world. We feel abandoned by God.

I'm sure that is how Joseph must have felt when he was in his black hole, at the bottom of a deep pit, with no way of escape. His black-hole despair must have deepened when his brothers sold him to the Midianite slave traders who bound him in chains and forced him to march across the desert with a lash at his back. Later, when Joseph was convicted of a crime he didn't commit and sat for years in an Egyptian jail, he must have wondered why God gave him dreams of a bright future only to abandon him to a terrible fate in an alien land.

A black hole is a living nightmare. It feels as if we have no control over any aspect of our life. The fear is constant. We see happy, smiling faces around us, and we know that no one understands how we feel. No one can comfort us in a black hole. We're totally alone.

I publish a daily e-mail devotional called *TGIF—Today God Is First*.[1] One day, I received a response from a *TGIF* subscriber who identified with the black-hole experience. This subscriber wrote:

> I'm sitting and crying as I read today's devotional. There's so much inside of me, and I don't know how to put into words the turmoil I'm going through. I have such a desire to experience the fullness of knowing and serving Jesus. I have so much love for Him and for His kingdom, yet I feel I don't fit in anywhere. I don't have a part to play in the Body of Christ.
>
> I feel like I'm dangling in mid-air, embracing but not being embraced, belonging but lost. I feel lonely and set apart, in love with Christ but disconnected from Him. It's as if I'm an alien even in my own church.
>
> So your message today was a blessing. I still can't see the bigger picture, but there is one, isn't there? I do have a purpose. God does have a plan for my life, a destiny for me to fulfill.
>
> I don't want to miss Him. So I die, I wait, I believe, I love, I trust, I live in Him. Thanks, Os, for your words of reassurance.

Like the writer of those words, you are probably full of questions as you go through your black-hole experience. But even as you question, hold on to God. Keep trusting Him. Wait, believe, love and know that He is at work in your life, even in the silence of your black hole. This is a season of preparation.

Angry at God

My Joseph Pit experience began when my then-wife said she wanted a separation. Three years into my seven-year trial, I was still fighting to stave off divorce. I had spent hours and hours in prayer, pleading with God to move on my behalf. But one day, the door slammed shut. It was my darkest day. Hadn't God heard my prayers? Didn't He care?

Feeling betrayed by God, I stormed out the door and walked up the heavily wooded hill behind my house. Reaching the hilltop, I raged at Him. "God!" I shouted, "Is this how You treat someone who is faithful to You? I've waited and waited. I've worked and prayed. And for what? For this?" My lungs hurt and my throat was raw—but I had one more thing to say to God: "I hate You, God! I hate You!"

I sat down on an old oak tree that had broken at the base and was lying on the ground. For the next three hours, I sobbed uncontrollably, unable to speak, unable to pray. I wondered how God could abandon me. I wondered if He even existed. Maybe I had wasted my life believing in a myth.

Finally, I got up to leave. When I looked over at the fallen oak that I had sat on, I noticed something interesting. The fallen tree was pointed toward the base of another oak tree—a tree that stood strong and tall with wide spreading branches. At that moment, I heard a quiet voice inside me say, *Today, like this broken oak tree, you are a broken man. But this brokenness was needed in order for you to become like the large, strong oak tree that stands before you.*

I walked down the hill, my mind whirling with questions. What was my life going to be like as a divorced man? Would I ever have a ministry for God again? Surely my Christian witness was nothing but smoke and ashes. I was a failure as a businessman, as a Christian, as a husband and as a father. And yet God had spoken to me, hadn't He? That quiet voice within me had promised that my broken life would stand tall and strong again. I didn't see how that promise could be fulfilled. I wasn't even sure that the promise had come from God. Maybe it was my own wishful thinking.

Years later, I would look back and know that God Himself had spoken to me out of the darkness and silence of my black hole. Today, whenever I read Isaiah 61, I am reminded of God's faithfulness to me. Speaking through the prophet Isaiah, the Lord promised to

> Provide for those who grieve in Zion—
> to bestow on them a crown of beauty
> > instead of ashes,
> the oil of gladness
> > instead of mourning,
> and a garment of praise
> > instead of a spirit of despair.
> They will be called oaks of righteousness,
> > a planting of the LORD for
> > the display of his splendor (Isa. 61:3).

Even in my black hole when I raged at God and told Him I hated Him, God was faithful and forgiving. Today, He has replaced the ashes of my despair with the oil of gladness. He has planted me firmly like a strong and sturdy oak tree, and I live my life in gratitude for His mercy. But this didn't happen overnight.

The Death and Resurrection of a Vision

During my black hole, a friend gave me a book by Oswald Chambers called *Not Knowing Where*. It became my life preserver. In the book, Chambers recounts the story of Abraham's journey into an unknown territory:

> God's method always seems to be vision first, and then reality, but in between the vision and the reality there is often a deep valley of humiliation. How often has a faithful soul been plunged into a like darkness when after the vision has come the test.[2]

We see this principle in the life of Joseph. God gave him a vision of being a ruler, but that vision died when his brothers tossed him into the pit. We see it in the lives of Jesus' disciples: Jesus told them that they would be leaders in His coming Kingdom, but that vision died when Jesus was nailed to the cross. The pattern is clear: First, God gives us a vision, and then that vision dies. Finally, God resurrects that vision in a new and amazing form.

We often become impatient in the black hole. The dream dies, and we are unwilling to wait for the resurrection, so we hurry things along. We see this in the life of Abraham. God gave Abraham a command and a promise:

> The LORD had said to Abram, "Leave your country, your peo-
> ple and your father's household and go to the land I will show
> you. I will make you into a great nation and I will bless you;
> I will make your name great, and you will be a blessing" (Gen.
> 12:1-2).

God gave Abraham a dream that his descendents would form a great nation. But for Abraham to have descendents, he must first have a son. As the years passed and Abraham's wife, Sarah, still did not bear a child, Abraham began to doubt God's promise.

At Sarah's suggestion, Abraham decided to help God fulfill His own promise. He had sexual relations with Sarah's maidservant, and the maidservant bore a son, Ishmael. But Ishmael wasn't the son God had promised; he was the son of Abraham's impatience. Later, God enabled Sarah in her old age to bear Abraham a son—Isaac, the son of God's promise.

When we try to do God's will in our own way and according to our own timetable, we are giving birth to Ishmael, not to Isaac. We are not living according to God's promise but according to our own impatience.

In 1996, when I was two years into my pit experience, I launched a new magazine called *Christians in Business*. I thought this magazine was my "promised son," my Isaac, the fulfillment of the dream God had given to me. I was wrong. The magazine died after two issues for lack of funding. After having already lost $500,000, I could hardly afford another big setback, but the *Christians in Business* debacle cost me another $50,000.

I was devastated and baffled. I felt that I was obediently following God's leading, yet my dreams continued to end in disaster. Today, I understand that the magazine was my Ishmael, not my Isaac. I was trying to do God's will according to my own timing. I was trying to hurry through the black-hole process instead of waiting on God.

When our vision dies, we often panic! We try to give our vision mouth-to-mouth resuscitation. We are too impatient and distrustful to simply wait and see how God is going to restore our dreams in His own time, by His own power. In *Not Knowing Where*, Oswald Chambers states:

> Whenever God gives a vision to a saint, he puts the saint in the shadow of His hand, as it were, and the saint's duty is to be still and listen. . . . When God gives a vision and darkness follows, waiting on God will bring you into accordance with the vision He has given if you await His timing. Otherwise, you try to do away with the supernatural in God's undertakings. Never try to help God fulfill His word.[3]

In the book of Proverbs, Solomon warns us not to rely on our own fallible wisdom while trying to do God's perfect will. He writes:

> Trust in the LORD with all your heart
>   and lean not on your own understanding;
> in all your ways acknowledge him,
>   and he will make your paths straight.
> Do not be wise in your own eyes;
>   fear the LORD and shun evil (Prov. 3:5-7).

God places us in black holes to teach us to trust Him with all our hearts—and that means He wants us to learn to trust His timing. God wants us to wait for His deliverance. Painful though it is, the black hole is God's gift to us. It is His means of bringing us to spiritual maturity so that we will be able to discern the difference between our own self-deliverance and God's authentic deliverance in our lives.

*It's a paradox, but it's true: God often calls us to a ministry and then deliber-
ately thwarts our efforts to achieve our goals!* We see it in Exodus 5 when Moses
met with Pharaoh. In obedience to God, Moses told Pharaoh, "Let my
people go!" How did Pharaoh respond? He said, "Who is the Lord, that I
should obey Him and let Israel go? I do not know the Lord and I will not
let Israel go." Again and again, Moses returned and demanded freedom
for his people. Again and again, Pharaoh refused.

So Moses complained to God, "You called me to go to Pharaoh, but
You are not freeing the people!" Moses grew discouraged because God
had called him to fulfill a vision—a dream of liberation for His people—
and the vision seemed to die. But God was teaching Moses and the people of Israel to wait and trust.

The Crisis That Defines Us

God may also place us in black-hole situations in order to give us a message to share with the world. Jesus said, "Whatever I tell you in the dark,
speak in the light; and what you hear in the ear, preach on the house-
tops" (Matt. 10:27, *NKJV*). Oswald Chambers reminds us that "song
birds are taught to sing in the dark" and that the darkness is not a place
for talking but a place for listening and learning. "If you talk to other
people," he says, "you cannot hear what God is saying. When you are in
the dark, listen, and God will give you a very precious message for someone else once you are back in the light."[4]

One way to look at a black hole is to see it as a *defining moment*. A defining moment is a time in our life when everything changes and we know
that there's no turning back. A defining moment crystallizes us and
shapes us into the kind of people we will be. It's an event in our lives that
gives form and meaning to our existence.

The defining moment in the life of Moses came when he heard God
call to him from a bush that burned but miraculously was not consumed. The defining moment for Daniel came when God delivered him
from the lions' den. The defining moment for Joshua came when the
Jordan River parted and he set foot in the Promised Land. The defining

moment for Peter came when by faith he stepped out of a boat and walked on water toward his Lord.

My defining moment was my black hole. That intense time of trial reshaped my thinking, transformed my relationship with God and redefined who I was as a Christian and as a businessman. It redirected the course of my life. My life has never been the same since then. I can never go back to being the man I was before—and I have never wanted to.

The longer I live, the more convinced I become that those whom God uses in a great way experience three stages of life. First, there is the life they live before their crisis with God. Second comes the crisis that defines them for the rest of their lives. Third comes their post-crisis life in which they live out the calling God has placed on their lives. Where are you in your journey?

Salvation is only the beginning of God's plan for our lives. He doesn't merely want us to be saved. He wants to use us in a mighty way as partners in His vast plan for restoring the universe from the effects of sin. But before He can use us, He must refine us and define us. Once we have experienced our defining moment, we will never be the same.

What to Do in a Black Hole

When we find ourselves in a black-hole experience, we shouldn't just sit and brood. We need to take stock of our life. We need to take a look at our relationship with God. *We need to take action!*

First, we must ask God if there are any sins, habits or attitudes that He might be judging in our life. When we go through adversity, it's important to discern whether the trial we face is the result of God's discipline for our sin or if it is preparing us for a future leadership role. We need to constantly make sure that our life is pure before Him. The Bible states that Satan has a right to sift us if there is sin in our lives (see Luke 22:31; 1 Cor. 5:5).

Second, we have to trust God when we enter a black hole. We can't trust our feelings, for they will tell us, "God has rejected you. Abandon hope. He has left you utterly alone." Feelings change; God never changes. Feelings come and go; God is always with us. His promise to us is the same today as it was in Joshua's day: "As I was with Moses, so I will be with you; I will never leave you nor forsake you" (Josh. 1:5).

Third, we must remember that our black-hole experience is not only intended to refine and define us but that it's also intended to influence and change the lives of hundreds or even thousands of other people. Our adversity is not just for us but also for others in our sphere of influence. Knowing this may not make the black-hole experience any less painful or lonely, but it may change our perspective and enable us to see beyond our own suffering.

Fourth, we need to ask God for the grace to endure this trial. We need to ask Him to enable us to learn the lessons of adversity. We shouldn't try to hurry the black-hole process along or try to deliver ourselves through our own efforts. Remember, when Joseph was in the depths of the pit, there was nothing he could do about it. He couldn't climb out, jump out, levitate out or talk his way out. All he could do was pray, wait upon the Lord, and learn the lessons of adversity.

Fifth, we must lean on God. Even when we don't feel like praying, we need to pray. Even when we don't feel like reading His Word, we need to read. Even when we don't feel like singing songs of faith, we need to sing. And when we pray, we shouldn't just talk but also *listen*. We need to be silent before God and listen for His still, quiet voice. We can't trust in natural reasoning or human wisdom. Logic told Abraham that his wife, Sarah, was too old to bear him a son, so he did the logical thing and had a baby with another woman—and that's where he went wrong. As the apostle Paul observed, "For the foolishness of God is wiser than man's wisdom, and the weakness of God is stronger than man's strength" (1 Cor. 1:25). We can't lean on our own understanding, but only on God.

Sixth, we must be alert to new truths and new perspectives. During a black-hole experience, God often leads us to amazing new discoveries. A black hole can be a storehouse of unexpected riches for the soul. As God tells us:

> I will give you the treasures of darkness,
>   riches stored in secret places,
> so that you may know that I am the LORD,
>   the God of Israel, who summons you by name (Isa. 45:3).

Bible teacher F. B. Meyer once observed, "Whenever you get into a prison of circumstances, be on watch. Prisons are rare places for seeing things. It was in prison that Bunyan saw his wondrous allegory and Paul met the Lord and John looked through heaven's open door and Joseph saw God's mercy. God has no chance to show His mercy to some of us except when we are in some distressing sorrow. The night is the time to see the stars."[5]

One good thing that came from my black-hole trial was that I began to write. I started producing the *TGIF—Today God Is First* daily devotionals. Today, those devotionals are read daily by hundreds of thousands of people around the world. Writing has become a central focus of God's work in me. If I had not gone through that experience, I wouldn't be an author today.

Seventh, we must live each day to the fullest. We can't live in the past or in the future. We must live in the moment that God gives us right now. Our time of deliverance will come according to God's schedule. Meanwhile, we need to be faithful in doing what God has given us to do and be content in the place where He has put us.

We shouldn't think of the black-hole experience as an optional add-on to our life—an extra blessing designed to make us better Christians. When we go through a trial of adversity, we need to understand that God is performing radical surgery on our life. The purpose of this surgery is not to destroy us but to give us a new heart. God is making a fundamental change in who we are and who we will be.

From Adversity to Destiny

We all avoid pain. We keep our medicine cabinets loaded with pain relievers. We couldn't imagine major surgery without an anesthetic. Because we are so averse to pain, we think that God must desire that we experience pain-free lives. After all, a *loving* God surely wouldn't want us to suffer pain, would He? Although God takes no pleasure in our pain, we have to acknowledge that He sometimes allows painful circumstances to occur in our lives in order to shape us and make us more like Christ.

I once came across the following poem written by an anonymous Confederate soldier. The lines of this poem express the soul of a man who has learned the lessons of a black-hole experience:

I asked God for strength, that I might achieve;
I was made weak, that I might learn humbly to obey.
I asked God for health, that I might do greater things;
I was given infirmity, that I might do better things.
I asked for riches, that I might be happy;
I was given poverty, that I might be wise.
I asked for power, that I might have the praise of men;
I was given weakness, that I might feel the need of God.
I asked for all things, that I might enjoy life;
I was given life, that I might enjoy all things.
I got nothing that I asked for but everything I had hoped for.
Almost despite myself, my unspoken prayers were answered.
I am, among men, most richly blessed.[6]

Do we trust God to lead us even though we can't see the pathway in front of us? Do we trust Him to be all-knowing, all-loving and all-powerful? Do we believe He does all things well? As Paul wrote, "Everything that does not come from faith is sin" (Rom. 14:23). That's why God leads us through the darkness and silence of the black hole.

Only in the darkness do we learn to walk by faith.

QUESTIONS FOR REFLECTION

1. Think of a time when you prayed and God didn't answer your prayers as you thought He should. How did that disappointing experience affect your faith?

2. Have you ever been angry with God? What did you say to Him? How do you think God responded to your expression of anger?

3. Do you ever feel that God owes you an explanation for the difficult or tragic experiences you've gone through?

4. Think of a recent major decision you made in your life. What was the basis for the decision you made? Was it based on trust in God's wisdom or reliance on your own logic and understanding?

5. Are you going through a black-hole experience right now? If so, you are probably eager (if not impatient) for this painful experience to end. What do you think might happen if you tried to remove yourself from this black-hole experience before God's timing?

Notes
1. For a free subscription to *Today God Is First,* please visit http://www.marketplace leaders.org/ and click "Subscribe to TGIF Daily Emails."
2. Oswald Chambers, *Not Knowing Where* (Grand Rapids, MI: Discovery House Publishers, 1957), p. 83.
3. Ibid.
4. Oswald Chambers, *My Utmost for His Highest: An Updated Edition in Today's Language,* ed. by James Reimann (Grand Rapids, MI: Discovery House Publishers, 1992), February 14 entry.

5. FR B. Meyer, *The Life of Joseph* (Lynnwood, WA: Emerald Books, 1995), p.45.

6. "Prayer of an Unknown Soldier," quoted in Austin Pryor, "Trusting God to Answer Our Prayers," *Crosswalk.com.* http://www.crosswalk.com/family/finances/1386973.html (accessed April 24, 2006).

4

THE DESERT PLACE

*Therefore I am now going to allure her; I will lead her
into the desert and speak tenderly to her.*

HOSEA 2:14

An ancient Arabian fable tells of three merchants who crossed the desert. In the daytime, they would pitch tents for shelter from the desert sun. When the stars came out, they would ride their camels in the cool of the night. At one point, the merchants crossed a dry riverbed under the stars.

"Halt!" said a voice from the darkness.

All three men jumped down from their camels and huddled in fear. "Who's there?" one of them said.

"Don't be afraid," said the voice in the dark. "I won't harm you if you do as I say. See those pebbles at your feet?"

By the dim starlight, the merchants saw thousands of pebbles in the riverbed.

"Each of you—pick up a pebble and put it in your pocket."

The three merchants obeyed. Each took a pebble from the riverbed.

"Now leave this place," the voice said, "and don't stop until daybreak."

The merchants mounted up. One said, "What's this all about?"

"I will only say this," the voice replied. "In the morning, you will be happy—and sad. Now, go!"

Baffled, the three merchants proceeded on their way. As they traveled, they wondered what the voice meant by saying that they would be both happy and sad.

When morning came, the merchants stopped. Each man pulled the single pebble from his own pocket and saw that it sparkled in the morning sunlight. The "pebbles" were precious gems. One man had a ruby, another an emerald, and the third a sapphire.

"Jewels!" one merchant said, his face shining with joy.

"Oh, no!" wailed the second. "There were *thousands* of jewels all over the riverbed! Each of us took only one! Why didn't we grab handfuls?"

"Look!" shouted the third, pointing behind them. A desert wind had whipped up, erasing their tracks. "We can never find our way back!"

The voice in the desert had spoken truly. The merchants were happy and sad. They had found wealth in the desert—but they could have taken more!

This parable reminds us of the desert places that we will all go through on our way to finding God's will for our lives. God leads us out into the wilderness and invites us to fill our pockets with the riches of His wisdom and grace. Tragically, we pick up only a pebble or two. A day will come when we look back and feel happy for the riches we have found—and sad that we didn't gather more.

Led by Love into the Desert Place

The desert holds a special place in God's Word. The Scriptures portray the desert as a place of inspiration and exaltation—a place where people met God in a powerful new way. King David wrote the 63rd Psalm while in exile in the Desert of Judah. He was hiding from his son Absalom, who wanted to replace him as king of Israel. David wrote:

> O God, you are my God,
>   earnestly I seek you;
> my soul thirsts for you,
>   my body longs for you,
> in a dry and weary land
>   where there is no water (Ps. 63:1).

The prophet Jeremiah also spoke of the desert as a place where God could be found:

Go and proclaim in the hearing of Jerusalem:
"I remember the devotion of your youth,
how as a bride you loved me
and followed me through the desert,
through a land not sown" (Jer. 2:2).

For Joseph, a deep pit in the desert was the first stop on a 13-year journey through desolation and despair. That 13-year desert experience served to break Joseph's self-will and self-confidence. It taught him that he could not control anything and that he needed to rely on God to manage the events in his life. Joseph's desert trial prepared him by scorching the youthful pride and arrogance out of his young life so that when he was 30 years old he could rule Egypt at Pharaoh's side in a spirit of humility and servanthood.

Before becoming king of Israel, David was a shepherd. Part of his training for leadership involved hand-to-claw combat with the beasts of the wilderness, including the lion and the bear. David tells us in Psalm 144:1, "Praise be to the LORD my Rock, who trains my hands for war, my fingers for battle." Elijah learned the principles of spiritual leadership while in the wilderness of Gilead. And Jesus was tempted and tested for 40 days in the desert before He began to preach.

The book of Hosea shows how God dealt with the people of Israel by putting them in a desert place. Israel had become wealthy and proud, and the people had forgotten the Lord and were worshiping the idols of Baal. So God sent the prophet Hosea to the people to tell them:

"I will punish her [the nation of Israel] for the days
    she burned incense to the Baals;
she decked herself with rings and jewelry,
    and went after her lovers, but me she forgot,"
    declares the LORD (Hos. 2:13).

When Hosea gave that prophecy, the nation was experiencing unparalleled peace and prosperity. Israel's greatest enemy, Syria, was defeated. The land was green with vineyards and fig orchards. The people lived in large homes and possessed ivory, gold and jewels. When Hosea came pronouncing God's judgment against Israel, the people thought he was crazy. But Hosea insisted that the Lord was telling Israel, "Therefore I am now going to allure her; I will lead her into the desert" (Hos. 2:14).

What is this desert that God spoke of? He was speaking in a metaphor of Israel's coming trial of arid desolation in exile. But God was not leading the people of Israel into the desert to *hurt* them. He was taking them there to *heal* them. Hosea continues:

> Therefore I am now going to allure her;
>   I will lead her into the desert and speak tenderly to her.
> There I will give her back her vineyards,
>   and will make the Valley of Achor [Trouble] a door of hope.
> There she will sing as in the days of her youth,
>   as in the day she came up out of Egypt (Hos. 2:14-15).

The prophet Hosea was describing the same principle that the apostle Peter would later speak of in the New Testament:

> And the God of all grace, who called you to his eternal glory in Christ, after you have suffered a little while, will himself restore you and make you strong, firm and steadfast (1 Pet. 5:10).

The people of Israel had forgotten their Lord, so He intended to take them out into the desert place. There He would meet with them, comfort them, restore them and turn their valley of trouble into a doorway to a bright future. Notice that God, speaking through Hosea, says, "I will lead her into the desert *and speak tenderly to her*" and that there in the desert, Israel would "sing as in the days of her youth." God would transform the hot, sandy desert into a place of lush vineyards and rejoicing.

A Place Called the Wasteland

Skip Moen, Ph.D., is an author, speaker and leadership consultant. I first met Skip through a mutual friend in the spring of 2005. He was once a millionaire businessman in the telecommunications industry, but then he lost it all and went through a Joseph Pit experience of his own. For a long time, he struggled with God, but his faith survived, and he realized God was calling him to a ministry of encouraging Christian leaders in the marketplace. Today, he writes a devotional, *Today's Word,* which can be found at www.studylight.org/devos/tw/. Here's an excerpt from one of Skip's devotionals about the desert places of our lives:

> For most of us, the idea of a wilderness recalls pictures of the Arizona desert or the Sahara or the Northern Territories. We think of a wilderness as a place where men cannot live. But what we really mean is that men cannot live in these places the way that we would like to live. This reveals something important about the wilderness, so important that the biblical wilderness is an essential part of God's message. The wilderness is the place where men encounter God and, at the same time, it is a place inhabited by demons. It is the place of God's revelation of the Law and it is the place of great temptation. It is the place of His call and the place of our rejection. . . . Many today do everything possible to avoid these places.

Skip Moen has been to the desert place. He knows what it's like to be alone with the desolation and silence. God leads us into the solitude of the desert place so that we can meet Him and hear Him speak.

In his book *The Dream Giver,* my friend Bruce Wilkinson calls the desert experience "the Wasteland." Bruce's book is a parable written in the tradition of John Bunyan's *Pilgrim's Progress.* It's the story of a man named Ordinary who leaves the Land of Familiar to pursue his Big Dream. Ordinary soon finds himself battling Giants in a place called the Wasteland. In a magazine interview, Bruce explained:

The wasteland is God's training ground. . . . There are half a dozen different things that God does to the person going through the wasteland. While there, you usually just spin your wheels. It's so discouraging. You feel like God's not hearing your prayers, He's not letting you break through. And the truth of it is, He is hearing your prayers, but He's not letting you break through.

The wasteland isn't caused by sin. . . . It's like when Joseph was in the prison those times. In neither case did he sin to go to prison. God brought him into prison and it was a long and difficult wasteland of preparation of his confidence, his capacity, his character—everything. And then, when the wasteland was over, he walked out and ruled the biggest and the most powerful nation in the world.[1]

Perhaps God has given you a dream, but now it seems that your dream has withered and died under the scorching desert sun. It seems that God has gone away and is not listening to your prayers. But I want you to know that your dream still lives. God is with you, even if you can't see Him, hear Him or sense His presence. He is leading you through the Wasteland. In His good time, He will bring you to a place of refreshment and restoration.

What is the desert place you are going through right now? It might be a broken marriage and a series of business setbacks, as it was for me. It might be a hospital room and a series of radiation treatments. It might be the agonizing loss of a loved one—a spouse, a parent, a friend or even a child. It might be a trial of being slandered, falsely accused or unfairly criticized. The desert can take many forms.

But God wants to turn your desert places into lush green valleys of blessing. He wants to provide cool water for your thirst and shade against the desert sun. "Privileged soul, come apart, hide yourself," St. Bernard of Clairvaux wrote. "With Jesus, escape into the desert! It is there that manna falls from Heaven. Go into the desert, ascend to the heart of God! What wonderful works the good Master will accomplish in your dear soul if He finds it alone with Him!"

In 1996, during my own desert time, I drove to the coast to fast and pray for three days. While I was alone and listening for God, He spoke to my spirit in a still voice and said, "I'm calling you into a key role in work-place ministry. You will be a leader in that movement." It was the last thing that I expected to hear God say. I was just barely keeping my head above water financially and emotionally. My life was in total chaos. I had no desire to start a ministry or take a leadership role in a movement—and I questioned whether it really was God's voice I heard.

Today, as founder and director of the International Coalition of Workplace Ministries, I can see that God had a much better future planned for me than I could have imagined. If I hadn't gone to a quiet place to listen for His voice, I would have missed hearing His promise for my life.

The Road to the Promised Land

As we have seen, Scripture uses Egypt as a symbol for slavery and toil. Egypt is our past. The Promised Land is our future. But there is a wilderness between the two. The road to the Promised Land always leads through the desert.

Moses spent 40 years in the wilderness of Midian before God called to him from a burning bush and told him to lead Israel out of Egyptian bondage. Those 40 years in the desert were part of his maturation process. It was there that Moses learned humility, obedience and faith. As a result of Moses' 40 years of desert preparation, the Bible says that he was "a very humble man, more humble than anyone else on the face of the earth" (Num. 12:3).

Moses obeyed God's call, led his people out of Egypt and through the Red Sea, and then he and his people wandered in the wilderness for *another* 40 years! *Sometimes God has to take us into the desert in order to get Egypt out of our system.* We have to experience a separation from our old lives in order to receive the new one that God has planned for us.

The Hebrew word for "desert" is *midbaar*, which comes from *dahbaar*, meaning "to speak." God called the people out of Egypt and into the desert so that they might hear Him speak. For some reason, God does not seem to speak to us until we have been in the desert for an extended period of time. Perhaps it's because it takes us a long time to reach a point where we're ready to listen.

In Deuteronomy 8, Moses explains to the people of Israel why God has led them into the desert:

> Be careful to follow every command I am giving you today, so that you may live and increase and may enter and possess the land that the LORD promised on oath to your forefathers. Remember how the LORD your God led you all the way in the desert these forty years, to humble you and to test you in order to know what was in your heart, whether or not you would keep his commands. He humbled you, causing you to hunger and then feeding you with manna, which neither you nor your fathers had known, to teach you that man does not live on bread alone but on every word that comes from the mouth of the LORD. Your clothes did not wear out and your feet did not swell during these forty years. Know then in your heart that as a man disciplines his son, so the LORD your God disciplines you (vv. 1-5).

Here, Moses reveals five reasons why God brought the people of Israel to a desert place. First, He led them there to humble them. Second, He led them there to test them. Third, He led them there so that they could experience His miraculous provision by receiving manna, the food of heaven. Fourth, He led them there to focus their minds on spiritual things—to teach them that human beings do not live on bread alone but on God's own Word. Fifth, He led them there to lovingly discipline them, just as a parent disciplines a child. God was taking the people of Israel from a state of childhood to a state of maturity. He did so by leading them through the desert place.

Provision in the Desert

In the desert, God teaches us an entirely new paradigm about His provision. When we are no longer able to earn a living for ourselves, we discover what it means to live by faith. When we can no longer defend ourselves, we find out what it means to let God be our strength and shield. In the desert place, we learn an important truth that can't be learned in any other place in life: *Jehovah Jireh*—God is our provider.

We can never know God's faithfulness in the material things in life until we are forced to rely totally upon Him. It's easy to say that we trust God to provide for our needs when we have thousands of dollars in our bank account. But that's not trust. We don't really learn what trust means until we reach a desert place in life and don't know where our next meal is coming from.

When God leads us into the desert, He often seems to dry up our resources for a season. We have no power to meet our own needs. Yet He always provides. God allowed the people of Israel to wander in the desert for 40 years—*yet their clothes and sandals did not wear out*. That's a remarkable manner of provision! It reminds me of how, during my own desert experience, God kept my 1993 Ford Explorer running for more than 230,000 miles.

Another way God provided for His people was with a miraculous substance called *manna* (see Exod. 16:31; Num. 11:7-8). It came in the form of small flakes that covered the ground like frost, and it had a flavor like flour mingled with honey and oil. The manna fell daily from heaven (except on the Sabbath) and was the staple of the diet of Israel during their 40-year desert sojourn. The manna had to be gathered in the morning, before the desert sun melted it, and it could be eaten in its natural state or baked into cakes. God commanded that each family gather only as much manna as could be consumed in a day (or two days' worth on the eve of the Sabbath).

God put a self-destruct feature in the manna: If anyone tried to gather more than a day's worth (except on the day before Sabbath), it would become putrid and full of maggots (see Exod. 16:20). The message here is clear: God was teaching the Israelites to trust Him for their provision—one day at a time. An Israelite who hoarded manna demonstrated that he didn't trust God to provide for him tomorrow and the next day.

I can identify with those Israelites who hoarded manna only to see it spoil. For many years, I thought that I was trusting God, yet I was hoarding earnings from my business ventures out of fear that I might run out of money someday. Yes, I tithed and gave money to the church, but I also made sure that I had plenty of money in the bank. I was not living by faith. I was living by fear.

The Lord decided that I needed to learn to trust in His provision alone, so He wiped out my finances. He emptied my investment accounts. God wants us to live by trust, not fear. When we operate by fear, the Lord will lovingly discipline us and teach us to trust Him.

It was a scary thing to see my business dry up. I had many obligations to banks and other businesses and I needed a significant cash flow to make my monthly payments. During this time, I concluded a profitable consulting contract with a client—and I had no prospects for replacing that income. But just as God provided manna in the wilderness, He provided the new income I needed.

I received a call from a new ministry, asking me to consult with them for the next year. The director of this ministry sensed God urging him to underwrite my entire salary out of his own pocket—a significant amount of money. Here was a source of provision that fell straight out of heaven like manna.

After a year, that contract came up for renewal and the ministry informed me that its financial commitment would be cut in half. Once again, I wondered where I would make up the lost income. Around that same time, I received a call informing me that a supporter had just placed $20,000 into my account. That gift was God's reassuring message to me: "Os, you have nothing to worry about. I'm still your Provider."

While I was in the middle of my seven-year Joseph Pit experience, God was working at a deep level in my life. He opened doors for me to speak to various marketplace groups. One group invited me to Barbados to speak to a small group of workplace leaders. I was not enthused about going. I knew that it would take two or three days of my time and that the honorarium would only be a few hundred dollars. I was so concerned about finances that I saw the event as a low-paid chore instead of an opportunity to serve God and others. But after praying about it, I realized that God was telling me to go, so I went.

As expected, the group was small, and so was the honorarium. I spent most of my time ministering to the leader, because he was going through a marriage crisis. Not wanting to lug my books back to the United States, I left most of them behind. I couldn't have predicted what happened next.

A man in Trinidad took one of the books I left behind. He read it, was excited about the message of the book, and called to ask me to speak at a large marketplace conference later that year. Attendees from 22 Caribbean islands came and listened to me give a workshop on the Joseph Calling. Afterwards, a man came up and told me how much the workshop had helped him. He was a successful business leader on one of the islands.

The following December, that same man attended a conference in Dallas at which I spoke. On January 2, I received a FedEx envelope from him with a check for $5,000. The man who had invited me to speak has since become a close personal friend and board member with our ministry.

I accepted a speaking engagement I didn't want to accept—and God brought blessing after blessing into my life. I learned a key lesson: *God's provision and blessing do not always come at the moment we act in obedience to His calling.* Sometimes, the blessings come later, magnified and multiplied by a chain of circumstances that we could never have predicted. When God leads us into the desert place, He doesn't leave us to die. He provides manna from heaven, and it sustains us day by day.

"Give Them Everything You Have"

My friend and mentor Gunnar Olson tells how he and his wife, Asther, experienced God's miraculous provision in their lives several years ago. One evening, they attended a prayer meeting in the home of a friend. It was a huge home, and there were about 100 people packed into the large living room. Gunnar found a corner where he could be alone to pray.

As he knelt, he had a vision. "I saw a family in front of me," he told me, "as if they were on a cinema screen. I saw everything about them: their names, their address, and their hopeless financial problems. I knew that the Lord wanted me to help them, so I asked the Lord what I should give them. To this day, I don't know whether I heard His reply with my ears or my heart. I only know that God said, 'Give them everything you have.'"

Gunnar had not expected that! God's message frightened him. He feared that he had become a religious fanatic. At the time, he was just weeks away from starting a new business. He needed every dollar of start-up capital he had. This was not the time to throw money away.

Gunnar got to his feet and went to another room, where Asther was looking after the children. He told her about his vision—and she looked shaken. But then she said, "Gunnar, we have been seeking God's direction for taking our financial ministry in a new direction. We want this ministry to be based not just on our ability to make money but also on obedience to God's Word. Perhaps this is God's way of moving us away from dependence on our own efforts and toward total dependence on Him. Blessing always comes through obedience. I'll fast and pray for a week."

So Asther fasted, prayed and asked God for a clear sense of His will. At the end of a week, she went to Gunnar and said simply, "Okay, let's do it."

The next day, Gunnar and Asther withdrew everything from the bank, pooled their pocket money, and even emptied the children's piggy banks. Then they drove to the address that Gunnar had seen in his vision.

"As I pulled up outside the house," Gunnar recalled, "I wondered how I was going to explain my visit. The words just tumbled out as soon as the door opened, and I stood looking at the family that I had seen in my vision. I said, 'Hello. I've come to bring greetings from a Friend. He wants you to know that He loves you and you're not alone.'"

Then Gunnar handed the family a large envelope containing the money. He and Asther said goodbye, got in their car, and drove away.

For the family that received the money, it was a turning point—but it was a more profound turning point for Gunnar and Asther. "The Lord knew what He was doing," Gunnar reflects. "Our savings had vanished, along with our comfort zone. Our lives had been altered. So Asther and I sat down at the breakfast table with my family and tried to explain our new situation with our two children, seven-year-old Mats and five-year-old Git. I said, 'You know that when you are hungry, you come to Mum and Dad and we give you food. Well, it's exactly the same with our Father in heaven. If we need anything, all we have to do is ask God and trust His love for us.' I told the children what we had done. Then I said, 'Now, let's talk to our Father in heaven. Out of His love for us, He will give us what we need for today.'"

What did Gunnar, Asther, Mats and Git pray for? Several very simple, basic things: butter, coffee, milk and two loaves of bread. After asking for those items, they thanked God that He had already provided for all of their needs in Jesus.

A couple of hours later, a neighbor appeared at the door. "I know this sounds silly," she said, "but I was in the city center, and they were selling bread so cheaply that I bought 10 loaves. It's too much for our needs. I wonder if I could give you four loaves?" She was offering twice as many loaves as they had prayed for!

Gunnar and Asther hadn't told a soul about their need or their prayer, yet God had sent bread to them by means of a neighbor lady. Before the day was over, the butter, coffee and milk had also arrived by unexpected means. The Olson family learned a powerful lesson that day: Jesus is real, and He's involved in our lives! He cares even about the simple, basic things in life.

This is just one of the many lessons that God wants to teach us by leading us into the desert place. Do not fear the isolation of the wilderness. Do not fear this school of preparation. You can trust God's provision for your life because His promise is sure:

They will neither hunger nor thirst,
    nor will the desert heat or the sun beat upon them.
He who has compassion on them will guide them
    and lead them beside springs of water (Isa. 49:10).

QUESTIONS FOR REFLECTION

1. Have you ever gone out into a desert, such as Death Valley in California or the Sonoran Desert in Arizona? Recall what it was like: the heat, the desolation, the silence. What were your feelings as you absorbed the mood of the desert?

2. Have you ever been to a desert place in your life? What were your emotions? What was your relationship with God like? What lessons did you learn about yourself and God in that desert place?

3. Describe a time in your life when God provided exactly what you needed by an unexpected or miraculous means. How did that provision affect your faith?

4. Reflect for a moment on the story of Gunnar and Asther Olson. What key lesson can you take away from their act of obedience and their experience of God's provision?

Note

1. Bruce Wilkinson, quoted by Ian Hodge, "How Your Dreams Can Become Your Life's Work," *Business Reform*, December, 2006. http://www.businessreform.com/article.php?articleID=11672.

PART II

SOME LEADERS ARE CALLED TO BE TESTED

TEST NO. 1: THE JUDAS TEST

*But Jesus asked him, "Judas, are you betraying the
Son of Man with a kiss?"*

LUKE 22:48

While going through the worst crisis of my career, I was put through a test that I call the Judas Test. This occurred at the time that I had just lost my biggest client (which represented 70 percent of our billings) and the vice president of my agency, whom I considered a close friend and Christian brother, had left the company and had taken my second-largest account.

As I mentioned, he had signed a non-compete agreement, and at first I had every intention of enforcing it. But after a great deal of prayer and counsel from Christian friends, I decided to release this man from the agreement. I told him that I didn't agree with what he was doing by violating his word to me, but that I would not hold him to the agreement.

My trusted friend had become my Judas. But I realized that after all that the Lord had forgiven me, I could not hold a grudge against this man. When Jesus said, "Love your enemies," He meant it.

I lost a friend and I lost the account, but God took care of me. In the process, I sensed Him speaking to my spirit and saying, "Os, you're beginning to grasp what I'm trying to teach you. I wanted you to release this man and leave the outcome in My hands. You've done that, and I'm pleased. You've passed the Judas Test."

Years later, this man came back to me and asked for my forgiveness. I told him that I had already forgiven him. Twelve years later, he found himself in his own Joseph process and came to me for counsel.

Whether the one who hurt us apologizes or not, what truly matters is that we obey God and forgive those who sin against us. When we forgive, we receive God's affirmation and approval.

An Overview: Joseph's Four Tests

God took Joseph through four specific tests. Although the Scriptures do not say so, I believe that Joseph had to pass each test before going on to the next. After passing one test, he was given another. When Joseph passed the fourth and final test, God elevated him to the second-highest leadership position in the land of Egypt. Once he was there, God used Joseph in a mighty way to achieve His purposes in history.

The first test Joseph faced was the Judas Test—a trial of being rejected and betrayed (just as Jesus was betrayed by Judas Iscariot). Joseph's Judas Test came when his brothers betrayed him, cast him into a pit and sold him into slavery. When Joseph refused to allow bitterness to rule his life, he passed the Judas Test.

Joseph's second test, the Integrity Test, came while he was working for Potiphar, an official of Pharaoh. Potiphar's wife tried again and again to seduce him, but Joseph steadfastly resisted her advances. A trial of temptation is one of the most difficult trials of all—and Joseph's trial was especially difficult because Potiphar's wife had a position of power and influence over Joseph's life. But by never succumbing to temptation, Joseph passed the Integrity Test.

Joseph's third test came as he spent years in prison after being falsely accused by Potiphar's wife. While he was in prison, Joseph did a favor for one of his cellmates by interpreting the man's dream. The man promised to help Joseph, but upon being released from prison, the man forgot about Joseph. For years, Joseph languished in prison, abandoned and alone. Joseph's test was one of being in a trial of adversity that seemed to have no end—the Perseverance Test. When Joseph passed this test, he was ready for the final test.

Joseph's fourth test was the Test of Success. It came when Pharaoh freed Joseph from prison and elevated him to a place of power and influence. Most of us would say, "Joseph became rich and powerful? What kind of test is that? How hard can that be? Lord, I'm ready to be tested by wealth and promotion anytime! Bring it on!" But the Test of Success is much more difficult than most of us imagine. Bible teacher Charles H. Spurgeon wisely observed:

> It is a dangerous thing to be prosperous. The crucible of adversity is a less severe trial to the Christian than the refining-pot of prosperity. . . . We are full and we forget God: satisfied with earth, we are content to do without heaven. Rest assured it is harder to know how to be full than it is to know how to be hungry—so desperate is the tendency of human nature to pride and forgetfulness of God.[1]

In this chapter, we will look at the first of Joseph's four tests—the Judas Test. We will examine the second, third and fourth tests in the next three chapters.

Joseph: A Type of Jesus

In the original Hebrew, the name "Joseph" means "God Will Increase" or "May God Add." But when Pharaoh brought Joseph out of the prison and gave him the position of second-in-command over Egypt, he gave Joseph a new name in the Egyptian language: Zaphnath-Paaneah (see Gen. 41:45). Joseph's Egyptian name has a profound meaning: "Savior of the World." If that sounds familiar, it's because *Joseph is a prophetic symbol of Jesus Christ.*

When we compare the life of Joseph to the life of Jesus, it is amazing how many symbolic parallels we find. Let's look at some of those parallels.

As just mentioned, Joseph's Egyptian name means "Savior of the World." Jesus' name means "the Lord Saves." When Jesus spent two days in a Samaritan village after His encounter with the woman at the well, the people of the village said, "We know that this man really is the Savior of the world" (John 4:42). And the apostle John wrote, "We have seen and testify that the Father has sent his Son to be the Savior of the world" (1 John 4:14).

Joseph was rejected by his own brothers; Jesus was also rejected by His own people. Joseph was betrayed and sold for 20 pieces of silver; Jesus was betrayed and sold for 30 pieces of silver. Joseph worked as a humble slave; Jesus came as a humble servant. When Joseph's brothers decided not to murder Joseph, they sold him into slavery and he was sent away to Egypt (see Gen. 37:28). When Jesus was a baby, he was taken to Egypt so that he would not be murdered by Herod (see Matt. 2:13).

Joseph was falsely accused by Potiphar's wife; Jesus was falsely accused at His trial. Joseph was innocent; Jesus was sinless. Joseph suffered at the hands of the Gentiles (the Egyptians); Jesus suffered at the hands of the Gentiles (the Romans). Both faced tests of being tempted. Both resisted the tempter and did not sin.

Joseph and Jesus were both 30 years old when they began their public ministries (compare Gen. 41:46 and Luke 3:23). Joseph and Jesus both had a prophetic ministry in which they foretold things to come. Joseph suffered on behalf of the brothers he later saved; Jesus suffered on behalf of all humanity, whom He later died to save. Joseph forgave his brothers, who threw him into the pit; Jesus forgave those who nailed Him to the cross. The Scriptures state that both Joseph and Jesus were filled with the Spirit of God (see Gen. 41:38; Luke 4:1).

Joseph saved an entire nation from starvation, and through him people from many nations were blessed (see Gen. 41:57). Jesus saved the world from sin, and through Him people from many nations were saved. Joseph gave bread to starving people; Jesus fed the multitudes and said, "I am the bread of life" (John 6:35).

God used Joseph in a prophetic way, shaping his life into an image of Christ. Joseph's life served as an Old Testament symbol of a New Testament reality. The life of Joseph was like a signpost pointing to the coming Messiah.

Before God could use Joseph as a prophetic symbol of Jesus the Messiah, God had to mold and shape this young man's character through adversity. Joseph had to be humbled. All the natural human pride and self-will had to be burned out of his soul. God was preparing Joseph for leadership.

Forgiveness: Graduate-Level Faith

Betrayal is one of the most difficult tests that we will ever face because it involves being wounded by someone we trust. It's hard not to become bitter when a friend or family member wounds us. It takes a lot of Christlike grace to forgive a traitor.

You have probably faced the Judas Test yourself. Every day, you and I work in a marketplace that is rife with betrayal, deception, duplicity and treachery. Perhaps you have been betrayed by your boss or a coworker. Or perhaps somebody betrayed a confidence or stabbed you in the back. It may have even been someone you've gone to church with or prayed with—someone you trusted as a brother in Christ.

The Judas kiss stings worse than a slap across the face. Almost every leader I know has experienced that sting at one time or another. Yet God is watching to see how we respond to the Judas Test. If we pass the test, He can then take us to the next level, the next test. If we fail, we'll probably have to repeat the test until we learn to forgive.

The Judas Test is God's graduate-level course in faith, designed to reveal the truth about ourselves: Are we willing to trust Him enough to forgive the Judases in our lives? The book of Hebrews warns, "See to it that no one misses the grace of God and that no bitter root grows up to cause trouble and defile many" (12:15). When we refuse to forgive those who betray us, we miss the grace of God—and we risk infecting others with a "bitter root" of resentment.

King David understood the pain of betrayal. He was subjected to the Judas Test several times throughout his life. In the psalms, he laments the betrayal he has suffered:

> If an enemy were insulting me,
>   I could endure it;
> if a foe were raising himself against me,
>   I could hide from him.

But it is you, a man like myself,
    my companion, my close friend,
with whom I once enjoyed sweet fellowship
    as we walked with the throng at the house of God (Ps. 55:12-14).

We cannot love and forgive our enemies in our own strength. This level of love requires graduate-level grace. Are we willing to enter this school of character building? Are we willing to undergo this test? God seeks to move us from one level to the next as He trains us and prepares us for greater use in His kingdom.

Women can be "Josephs" too! (Or should we call them "Josephines"?) Mary Whelchel, who hosts the daily radio program *The Christian Working Woman* (www.christianworkingwoman.org), tells the story of a Christian businesswoman who went through the Judas Test and demonstrated graduate-level faith:

American-born Sally Johnston lived in Switzerland and worked in a large bank in Zurich. After 10 years with that company, she rose to a responsible position in international banking. Her abilities were recognized by her superiors, coworkers and clients. Finally, she was appointed manager of a project that offered an exciting new opportunity in global banking—until her new boss decided he wanted this plum job for himself. He pushed her out of the project and took it over. He also took away every other challenging work assignment and excluded her from strategy sessions and customer contacts.

Sally struggled with resentment. She had her dreams and goals, but her boss had shot them down. For a talented, accomplished young woman, it was a bitter pill.

As Sally began looking for another position, she felt God urging her to forgive her boss and trust Him to deliver her from the situation. Finally, she went to God in prayer and said, "All right, God, I know I need to let go of this resentment. Please help me to forgive him. But I still don't understand why this is happening to me!"

In time, Sally was offered a new position within the bank—a job that she could approach with enthusiasm and optimism. After about a year in her new job, Sally heard that the global banking project she had wanted so badly was running months behind schedule and millions over budget. It wasn't because her former boss was incompetent, but because the project turned out to be "Mission Impossible."

Sally breathed a prayer of thanks to God that she had been cheated out of that assignment. If she had received what she wanted, it might have ruined her career! God had used an act of betrayal to save her from a career mistake. What had seemed like a curse was actually a blessing!

Convinced that God wanted her to use her position in the business world as a platform for Christian witness, Sally started a weekly Bible study for women. As a result, many other women in Sally's sphere of influence have been drawn into a vital and growing relationship with Jesus Christ. Why was Sally Johnston given this opportunity for leadership and ministry? I believe it's because she passed the Judas Test. When mistreated by her boss, she chose to respond with forgiveness and grace.

A bitter and unforgiving spirit has disqualified many a talented, gifted person from moving on with God. *He will not elevate us if there is any root of bitterness in our lives.*

Turning Weakness into Strength

The day after the first Marketplace Leaders Summit in Atlanta in 1997, Gunnar Olson and I had breakfast together. Gunnar knew that I was going through several Judas Tests at the time. "Os," he said, "just as Abraham's inheritance was the land, your inheritance is relationships. You connect people to people. I've tried to bring Christian business leaders together for years without success, but God used you to make it happen at this summit. You have a patriarchal call upon your life. You're a workplace apostle whom God uses to convene people for Kingdom purposes.

"But you must be especially careful in maintaining relationships. *Satan will always tempt you in the place of your inheritance.* Satan attacked Abraham by provoking Lot to take the better land. Abraham chose the higher road by allowing Lot to take the good land and by not holding a grudge. Satan is using these Judases in your life to attack you in the area of your inheritance: relationships. So you must choose the higher road by letting go of any bitterness toward those who have betrayed you."

I often recalled that counsel as I went through my Judas Tests, and it helped me to persevere in forgiving those who had hurt me.

Let's take a closer look at the story of Abraham and Lot, which is found in Genesis 13. One day, Abraham and his nephew Lot realized that the land they lived on could no longer support both families and their flocks. They would have to split up. But who should get first choice of the land?

As Lot's senior, Abraham had the right to make that choice. But that wasn't the approach Abraham took. Instead, he told Lot, "You choose. I'll abide by whatever you decide." Abraham knew full well that he might be dooming himself and his family to an arid, rocky land that couldn't sustain them. Although he had a right to take the best, Abraham gave up his rights—and Lot took full advantage!

Abraham's greedy nephew saw the green, rich, well-watered plain of the Jordan River gleaming like a garden of the Lord, and he took it. He moved his flocks into a beautiful little valley, and then took up residence in a nearby town. The name of that town was Sodom. Yes, *that* Sodom—the wicked city that God destroyed with fiery judgment.

Sometimes, what seems good in the present turns out to be disastrous later. Tragically, that would be the case for Lot and his family. Abraham, by contrast, chose to take the high road. He chose righteousness over selfishness and was willing to leave the outcome to God. Abraham could have bargained from a position of strength. Instead, he deferred to his nephew. Many people would call that a sign of weakness on Abraham's part. He had the advantage; he should have pressed it.

However, by adopting the "weak" position, Abraham's position became one of strength. Eventually, Lot and his family had to leave everything behind and flee the destruction of Sodom. Abraham was secure in the land that Lot walked away from. Lot's strength became his downfall. Abraham's weakness became his strength.

That's the paradox of the Christian life. As the apostle Paul states, "That is why, for Christ's sake, I delight in weaknesses, in insults, in hardships, in persecutions, in difficulties. For when I am weak, then I am strong" (2 Cor. 12:10).

Is a cross of execution a place of strength? Did Jesus seem strong when He was nailed to the cross, pinned in place by iron nails, writhing in agony as His life drained from His veins? Obviously not. Yet that is the place where Jesus defeated death and Satan. He was never stronger than when He was at His weakest.

What was true of our Lord is true of us: When we give up our rights and our resentment and allow God to work as He sees fit, our weakness becomes our strength.

What to Do When You Wrong Someone Else

Forgiveness should not be confused with reconciliation. There are times of conflict in our lives when it's impossible and even undesirable to be reconciled with the person who hurt us. There are some people who choose to be evil and destructive in all of their dealings. It's not healthy for us to remain in a relationship with such people. But neither is it healthy to remain bitter. For our own sake and for Jesus' sake, we must forgive them—and then move on.

At other times, there are differences and conflicts that just cannot be resolved. It doesn't mean that one person or the other is evil or sinful. It just means that the difference of opinion or the personality clash has no solution.

We see an example of this in the relationship of Paul and Barnabas, two partners in Christian ministry who had a sharp disagreement regarding a young man named John Mark. In Acts 15, we see that Barnabas wanted to take John Mark on a missionary journey. However, Paul refused. John Mark had disappointed him once before and Paul didn't want to give him another chance. In the end, Paul and Barnabas agreed to disagree—and to part company. Paul went one way;

Barnabas and John Mark went another. Sometimes, that's the only solution to a disagreement.

There's a postscript to this story: In 2 Timothy 4:11, Paul writes from his prison cell in Rome and tells Timothy, "Get Mark and bring him with you, because he is helpful to me in my ministry." Sometime after the disagreement between Paul and Barnabas, John Mark redeemed himself and became a valued partner in Paul's ministry. In fact, as Paul faced execution in Rome, he wanted his friend John Mark at his side.

Let me share with you two experiences that I went through in which I felt God calling me to forgive even though reconciliation proved difficult. In chapter 1, I told how, at the beginning of my Joseph Pit experience, my advertising agency suffered a major financial loss when our largest client refused to pay a bill for $140,000. About six months after that incident, I called a staff meeting to analyze our business dealings and make sure we were operating according to Christian standards. I wanted to know if the company or I had wronged any client or vendor. I invited John, a friend and mentor, to take part in the discussion.

We met and evaluated case after case. Near the end of the day, Anne, a recently hired secretary, asked, "What about the company that refused to pay the bill for $140,000?" It's interesting that God used Anne to raise a subject that hadn't come up all day. This taught me that everyone in the organization—even the "lowest on the totem pole"—should have a say.

I briefly explained the situation to my mentor, John. Our client had refused to pay the bill because of a dispute over a printing project. I felt that we had done all we could do to satisfy the client, but to no avail. I finally filed suit against the former client because we had been stuck with more than $40,000 in vendor costs for products the client was using but not paying for. To me, it was an open and shut case.

But John pointed out a flaw in my thinking. The real culprit was a manufacturer that I had contracted with to produce a product for the client. The manufacturer had delivered an inferior product. My complaint was really against the manufacturer, not the former client. The client wasn't entitled to use the product without paying for it, but he was entitled to a reasonable concession. The fact that the client was acting unreasonably had blinded me to the client's legitimate complaint, which was why I had felt justified in filing suit.

John told me that I wasn't justified at all. "You've got to drop your suit against him," he said. "And you need to ask his forgiveness." I defended my actions, but John insisted I was wrong. It took me a while to see his point, but in the end I knew he was right. I had been blind and stubborn, and God had used John to show me that I had some fence-mending to do. With John at my side, I called my attorney and said, "I want to drop the lawsuit."

My attorney was stunned. "Os," he said, "it's too late for that! Your client has already filed a counter suit. If you drop the suit now, you'll be completely exposed. On top of all the money you've lost, you'll be liable for hundreds of thousands more! Tell them you'll drop your suit if they drop theirs. I think we can still get $20,000 from them."

I looked at John. He shook his head and silently mouthed, "Drop the suit."

"I want to drop the suit regardless of what they will or won't do," I said.

My attorney sighed. "It's your funeral," he said.

My next move was to talk to my former client. I tried phoning him, but he wouldn't return my calls. Finally, I got his secretary and said, "I want you to take this message down and give it to your boss, word for word—no changes: 'I have sinned against you. I know that I don't deserve your forgiveness, but I ask your forgiveness for filing the lawsuit against you. You are no longer obligated to pay the balance you owe me if you don't feel you owe it.'"

I could hear the secretary begin to cry on the other end of the line. She couldn't believe what she was hearing. About an hour later, my former client called. We hadn't spoken for six months.

"My secretary said you called," he said.

"Did she give you my note?" I asked.

"Yes."

"I misjudged the situation. I've already dropped the suit. I'll pay the vendor costs out of my own pocket. I want to ask your forgiveness."

"I must admit that I'm troubled by your note."

"Troubled? Why?"

"I don't like to see a man get punished by God like this."

I didn't understand why he saw my apology that way. "I don't see this as punishment from God," I said. "He's given me the grace to see that I was blind. I'm making this decision of my own free will. Does this mean you're forgiving me?"

"Yes," he said. "I forgive you."

He dropped his counter suit. A few days later, I went to see him, and we had dinner together. It was a cordial evening, but his position on the disputed bill remained unchanged. He never offered to pay a dime of it, not even the expenses I had incurred. It took me five years to pay the vendors out of my own pocket.

The next few years were incredibly difficult because of the financial setback I suffered, but God provided for my needs. Looking back, I realize that this was my Judas Test. I passed the test when I let go of my resentment and asked to be forgiven, and God was glorified in the situation.

There were other Judas Tests that God brought into my life. For example, there was a man who had become a friend and mentor to me, but a conflict arose between us that we were unable to resolve. I never imagined that this man would go from being one of my best friends to an enemy. I asked God to show me how I should treat this man, and the words of Jesus came to mind: "Love your enemies and pray for those who persecute you" (Matt. 5:44).

"Lord," I said, "surely You don't mean I'm to love this man! Not after the way he's hurt me and refused to reconcile!"

As I argued with God, I remembered that Jesus, before He was betrayed, got down on His knees and washed the feet of Judas Iscariot, His enemy. The moment that scene came to my mind, I knew what God was calling me to do. I had to wash the feet of my Judas.

This man who had been my friend and mentor had also been a client of my advertising agency. He was a Christian author and speaker, and I decided to bless this man by continuing to promote his ministry and his books.

Did he ever come back to me and reconcile? Yes—seven years later. But even if he had never reconciled with me, I knew that I did what God called me to do. I washed the feet of my Judas. I passed the test.

God doesn't promise that if we forgive there will be a happy ending. He doesn't promise that the man who refuses to pay will suddenly write a check. He doesn't promise that the one who rejects reconciliation will instantly soften his heart. Jesus forgave His executioners, but that didn't keep them from nailing Him to the cross.

The Judas Test is not about getting the results we want. It's about proving that we trust God enough to forgive our Judases. It's a graduate-level course in Christian obedience. But I believe that every leader whom God uses in a significant way must pass the Judas Test.

God wants to know if we are willing to be imitators of Jesus the Master. How can we say we are followers of Christ if we won't wash the feet of our Judases?

QUESTIONS FOR REFLECTION

1. Do you think it was easy or difficult for Joseph to forgive his brothers for betraying him and selling him into slavery? Did it take him weeks, months or years to forgive them? Explain your answer.

2. A. W. Tozer said, "It is doubtful whether God can bless a man greatly until he has hurt him deeply." Why do you think this is so? How does this make you feel about God?

3. Paul said, "I delight in weaknesses, in insults, in hardships, in persecutions, in difficulties. For when I am weak, then I am strong" (2 Cor. 12:10). Do you seek to let God work His strength through your weakness? Or do you have to be strong in everything you do—in your finances, your relationships, your reputation, your conflicts and arguments, and so forth?

4. Why is forgiveness different from reconciliation? How is it possible to forgive without reconciling?

5. Is there a Judas in your life? Have you forgiven your Judas? Have you washed the feet of your Judas? Why or why not?

Note

1. Charles Haddon Spurgeon, *Morning and Evening* (New Kensington, PA: Whitaker House, 2001).

Test No. 2: The Integrity Test

No temptation has seized you except what is common to man.
And God is faithful; he will not let you be tempted beyond what you
can bear. But when you are tempted, he will also provide a
way out so that you can stand up under it.

1 CORINTHIANS 10:13

"I'll never forget the time I saw my first piece of pornography," recalls Dr. Gary Oliver, author of *Made Perfect in Weakness* and a professor of psychology and practical theology at John Brown University in Arkansas. "I was an eighth-grader at Hill Junior High. I was sitting in the library, working on a reading assignment when my friend Carl came over and sat next to me. He looked around and, in a very low voice, asked if I wanted to see something."

Carl pulled out a pornographic magazine. "My dad has a bunch of these at home," Carl said. "I'll sell you this one for 50 cents."

Gary bought it. He knew that lust was a sin, but he rationalized that at least it wasn't as bad as lying or stealing. It was just a harmless magazine!

"But it wasn't harmless," Gary laments. "What happened that day fueled what was to become a lifelong struggle with lust, sensuality and impurity. It followed me into high school, through college and seminary, and, at times, has even followed me into the present. Most of the time,

I've had victory over these temptations. But there have been times when I allowed a thought of a quick and 'harmless' thrill to become overwhelming. And each time, without exception, that promised pleasure has been engulfed by guilt, shame and sorrow."

The Integrity Test is the second of the four tests that Joseph underwent. It is a test that is especially difficult in our sex- and greed-saturated society, but one that we must all pass successfully in order to be used greatly by God. I can't imagine a harder test of temptation than the one Joseph faced. He stood his moral ground and paid the price.

The Bible tells us, "Blessed is the man who perseveres under trial, because when he has stood the test, he will receive the crown of life that God has promised to those who love him. When tempted, no one should say, 'God is tempting me.' For God cannot be tempted by evil, nor does he tempt anyone; but each one is tempted when, by his own evil desire, he is dragged away and enticed. Then, after desire has conceived, it gives birth to sin; and sin, when it is full-grown, gives birth to death" (Jas. 1:12-15).

Are you and I willing to make a stand against temptation? Are we willing to pay the high price of keeping our minds and bodies pure?

Joseph and the Integrity Test

After Joseph was sold into slavery by his brothers, he was purchased by Potiphar, a high-ranking Egyptian official. After watching how Joseph conducted himself, Potiphar placed the 17-year-old Hebrew youth in charge of everything he owned. Like any healthy, normal teenager, Joseph had plenty of male hormones surging in his bloodstream. As a slave, he probably didn't have much contact with the opposite sex.

Suddenly, the boss's wife was trying to seduce him! Since Potiphar was a rich and powerful man, we can assume his wife was attractive. So here was this hot-blooded teenager with a beautiful older woman coming on to him. His trusting boss was gone all day—so who would know? That's quite a temptation.

But when Potiphar's wife tempted Joseph, he replied, "My master has withheld nothing from me except you, because you are his wife. How then could I do such a wicked thing and sin against God?" (Gen. 39:9).

That's the voice of integrity. That's a young man of character taking a moral stand against temptation. And remember, this woman didn't just tempt him once. The Scriptures tell us, "And though she spoke to Joseph *day after day*, he refused to go to bed with her or even be with her" (v. 10, emphasis added). Joseph had to stand firm against *repeated* attempts to wear down his resistance.

Understand, too, that Joseph was being *sexually harassed* by a woman who had power over his life. One day when no one else was around, Potiphar's wife grabbed Joseph by his robe and said, "Come to bed with me!" She was through being subtle and decided to simply drag him into her bed. Joseph did the only thing a person should do when confronted by temptation: *He fled.* In his haste, however, he left his robe in her hand.

When Potiphar returned home, his wife showed him the robe and said, "That Hebrew slave you brought here came to me and tried to use me for his plaything! I screamed for help and he ran out of the house!" So Potiphar sent Joseph to prison.

How was Joseph rewarded for maintaining his integrity? He was slandered and falsely imprisoned. We live in a fallen world, and that's how the world often works. Sometimes, the righteous pay a high price for their integrity—but that's what the Integrity Test is all about. Before God elevates us to a position of leadership, He wants us to prove that we are willing to pay the price for doing His will.

The Temptation of Judah

In Genesis 38, we read how Judah, one of Joseph's brothers, allowed his purity—and the staff that represented his stature and position in the community—to be taken from him. This story shows how yielding to temptation can destroy a man's reputation and his witness for God.

The tale of Judah's temptation seems strange today because it involves cultural practices that are quite foreign to us. The significance of the story is underscored by its placement in the Bible: It interrupts the story of Joseph. In Genesis 37, we read of Joseph being cast into a pit and then sold into slavery. In Genesis 39, we read of Joseph in Egypt and his temptation by Potiphar's wife. But in between Genesis 37 and 39, we find this disturbing story of Joseph's brother Judah. Some Bible scholars believe that the story was placed where it was to show how Judah's sin contrasted sharply with Joseph's virtue.

Judah is the one who talked the other brothers out of murdering Joseph. It was his idea to sell Joseph as a slave. Perhaps Judah had pangs of conscience about what he and his brothers had done. In any case, Judah moved away from his other brothers and married a Canaanite woman, Shua. They had three sons: Er, Onan and Shelah.

Er, Judah's firstborn, married a Canaanite woman named Tamar. But when Er committed a terrible (but unspecified) sin, God put Er to death. The law of the time stated that if a man died childless, his brother was to marry the widow and produce children in his memory. (This was the law of "levirate marriage," as set forth in Deuteronomy 25:5-10.) The children born from this union would legally be the children of the dead man and would carry on his name.

So Judah told his middle son, Onan, "Lie with your brother's wife and fulfill your duty to her as a brother-in-law to produce offspring for your brother." Onan was willing to engage in sex with Tamar, but he didn't want to produce any offspring with her. As the oldest living son of Judah, he stood to inherit the bulk of Judah's estate. But if he impregnated Tamar, her children would inherit much of Judah's estate—and Onan's share would be reduced. So when Onan had sex with Tamar, he practiced *coitus interruptus* to prevent Tamar from getting pregnant. For cheating Tamar, God put Onan to death as well.

That left only Shelah, Judah's third-born. At this point, Judah became afraid of Tamar. Er was married to her, and he had died. Onan had sex with her, and he had died. Judah figured there was something dangerous about Tamar—perhaps a Canaanite curse. Judah didn't understand that his first two sons had died because of their own wickedness.

Fearing that Tamar would cause his third son to die, Judah kept Shelah away from Tamar, in violation of the law. Tamar was deprived of having children in memory of her husband. Under the law, Judah did a great injustice to his daughter-in-law. Although Tamar lived in Judah's house, Judah withheld his son from her.

So Tamar devised a plan to get what was hers. Hearing that Judah planned to go to the town of Timnah, she disguised herself with a veil and hurried to the village of Enaim, on the road to Timnah. She posed as a Canaanite prostitute and waited for Judah to pass by. Soon, Judah came up, saw a prostitute sitting at the gate, and propositioned her.

"What will you give me to sleep with you?" Tamar asked.

"I'll send you a young goat from my flock," Judah said.

Tamar said, "Give me something as a pledge—*your personal seal and the staff in your hand.*" The staff was the symbol of Judah's position in the community. The seal was a device for making an official impression in wax. It was, in effect, his I.D.—the Old Testament equivalent of a driver's license. So Judah gave her the staff and the seal with its cord. He slept with Tamar, and she got what she wanted all along. She became pregnant.

Judah went on his way and had a friend take a young goat to Enaim with instructions to find the prostitute and trade the goat for the seal and staff. The friend searched all over Enaim but couldn't find the prostitute. Hearing this, Judah became nervous. If word got out that he'd visited a Canaanite prostitute, he'd be humiliated.

Time passed and word reached Judah that Tamar was pregnant. Judah knew that there was only one way this could have happened: She had prostituted herself! Enraged, Judah said, "Bring her out and have her burned to death!"

As the people brought Tamar out to be executed, she cried out, "I am pregnant by the man who owns these!" She held in her hands the seal and staff of Judah. Seeing them, Judah knew he stood convicted. He broke down and confessed, "She is more righteous than I am!"

Judah had wronged Tamar by withholding his son and he had committed the sin of visiting a prostitute. Now he was publicly disgraced. The whole community saw the evidence of his sin. Tamar was spared—but the stigma and shame of Judah's sin would remain on him for the rest of his life.

That's what sexual sin does to a man. It drags his reputation into the gutter. It destroys his Christian witness and disqualifies him from ministry for God. Sin can take everything away from a man: his reputation, his career, and even his family.

This is why we dare not fail the Integrity Test. In recent years, the Christian Church has been barraged by scandal after scandal. Each time a Christian leader falls, lives are ruined, ministries are damaged, and the name of Christ is disgraced. No matter how strong we think we are, no one is immune to temptation.

The Enemies Without, the Traitor Within

This is a battle—and our enemy doesn't play fair. In fact, we face three enemies—two enemies without and an enemy within: the world, the flesh and the devil. The world and the devil are the enemies without. The flesh is the enemy within.

The devil is a spiritual adversary who seeks to destroy us. He is at war with God, and our soul is the battlefield. The world is the culture around us—the godless business system (which uses sex-laden advertising to sell every product from hamburgers to sports cars), the immoral arts and entertainment system, our worldly peers, and so forth. The flesh is that complex array of natural drives and appetites that have become distorted because of our fallenness as children of Adam and Eve.

The devil and the world have teamed up to attack us relentlessly from the outside. The world bombards us with constant messages of sex, selfishness and greed. Satan continually whispers to us, "Yield. Give in. You deserve it. It's only natural to want it." And the flesh? That's the traitor inside that continually tries to betray us to the enemy without. In *Wild at Heart,* John Eldredge says that this traitor seeks to surrender the castle of our souls to Satan. He writes:

> Stand on what is true and do not let go. Period. The traitor within the castle will try to lower the drawbridge but don't let him. . . . As Thomas à Kempis says, "Yet we must be watchful, especially in the beginning of the temptation; for the enemy is then more easily overcome, if he is not suffered to enter the door of our hearts, but is resisted without the gate at his first knock."[1]

Though God watches to see if we will pass the Integrity Test, God Himself is not tempting us. Satan is the tempter, not God. The Bible tells us:

And remember, no one who wants to do wrong should ever say, "God is tempting me." God is never tempted to do wrong, and he never tempts anyone else either. Temptation comes from the lure of our own evil desires. These evil desires lead to evil actions, and evil actions lead to death (Jas. 1:13-15, *NLT*).

We see how true those words are in the story of King David's moral failure. A seemingly insignificant choice in David's life ultimately led to adultery and murder. Here is how the Bible describes the beginning of David's downfall:

One evening David got up from his bed and walked around on the roof of the palace. From the roof he saw a woman bathing. The woman was very beautiful (2 Sam. 11:2).

David was walking on the roof of his palace when he noticed a woman bathing below. That was the moment of temptation. He could have turned his back and walked away, but he didn't. Instead, he did what so many of us do today with the cable TV remote or some after-hours Googling: David lusted after a naked woman. He engaged in voyeurism.

David probably rationalized it to himself, saying, "There's no harm in looking." He had no idea that the "harmless" lust he was indulging in would eventually leave a stain on his reputation that would be spoken of for thousands of years.

King David's problem started with looking at a nude woman, but it didn't end there. Even after the woman got out of the bath and went inside, he couldn't stop thinking of her. The more he thought about her, the more he had to have her. So David sent for the woman and began a torrid affair.

The woman, Bathsheba, became pregnant by King David while her husband, Uriah, a captain in David's army, was away on the battlefield. Because of the timing of the pregnancy, everyone would know that Uriah wasn't the father—and David's sin would be exposed. After trying and failing to cover up his sin, David ordered that Uriah be murdered on the battlefield.

Now we see the progression of sin in the life of a leader. David began with a seemingly insignificant lapse of integrity—a little voyeurism, a few moments of lust. From lust, he proceeded to adultery, and then to lies and cover-ups. Finally, David's sin led to murder.

James tells us, "Temptation comes from the lure of our own evil desires. These evil desires lead to evil actions, and evil actions lead to death" (1:14-15, NLT). It starts with a seemingly minor sin. It ends in shame and brokenness. We need to remember this whenever we think, *It's only a little pornography.*

It's not a sin to be tempted. It's only a sin to *give in* to temptation. But the challenge of temptation has probably never been worse than it is today. In our media-saturated world, the vilest pornography can be viewed with a few computer mouse-clicks. Like Potiphar's wife, sexual temptation comes to us day after day, trying to wear down our resistance, saying, "Come to bed with me! Come to bed with me!"

If a man like King David could fall so far because of temptation, what hope do you and I have? Actually, we have everything we need to defeat temptation. As the apostle Paul wrote, "No temptation has seized you except what is common to man. And God is faithful; he will not let you be tempted beyond what you can bear. But when you are tempted, he will also provide a way out so that you can stand up under it" (1 Cor. 10:13).

We *can* pass the Integrity Test. We just need a strategy for defeating temptation when it comes our way.

How to Pass the Integrity Test

Here is a seven-step strategy for winning over temptation. Follow this biblical strategy and you *will* experience victory over the world, the flesh and the devil.

Step 1: Start with a Commitment

Make a vow to yourself, to God, and to your spouse that you will not yield to the temptation. Draw a line in the sand—and then refuse to cross it. Don't rationalize. Don't make the mistake that King David made of allowing your gaze to linger on temptation.

Step 2: Share Your Commitment with Another Person

Ask a trusted friend to hold you accountable for the decision you've made. Join or start a group in your church to study the Bible, pray together, and be accountable to one another. You don't have to share every gory detail of your struggle, but be candid with people you can trust and invite them to regularly ask you how you are doing in the battle against temptation.

Step 3: Be Aware of the Stress That Triggers Temptation

In *Experiencing Spiritual Breakthroughs*, Bruce Wilkinson says that he finds temptation the greatest during times of stress. So he came up with a prayer that he calls a "Three-Minute Temptation Buster." He directs this prayer to the Comforter (the Holy Spirit), saying, "Dear Holy Spirit, You've been sent to me to be my personal Comforter. I am in desperate need of comfort. I don't want to sin. Please comfort me. In Jesus' name, Amen."[2]

Wilkinson says that the first time he prayed this prayer in a time of temptation, he checked his watch to see what would happen. He recalled, "Slowly, I became aware of something—I was comforted. My soul felt soothed and no longer in pain. When I turned back toward that temptation, I discovered it had miraculously slithered into the darkness, far away from my senses. I was free."[3] Since then, whenever he has prayed that prayer, the Holy Spirit has relieved his stress in three minutes or less.

Step 4: Flee Temptation; Never Compromise or Flirt with Sin

"Flee the evil desires of youth," wrote Paul in 2 Timothy 2:22. If you know that there are certain forms of temptation you can't resist, get them out of your life! Pull the plug on the Internet and on cable TV. Web-surfing and R-rated movies are not a necessity; godliness is.

Step 5: Remember the Terrible Cost of Sin

Remind yourself of the shame that sin produced in the lives of Judah and King David. Remember that you will one day have to give an account of your life to God (see Rom. 14:12). Remember that David's sin became a generational sin that affected the lives of his children. The risk is too great. The cost is too high. Don't give in to the thing that wants to destroy you.

Step 6: Meditate on God's Word

Psalm 119:11 tells us, "I have hidden your word in my heart that I might not sin against you." When Jesus was tempted in the desert, He responded to each satanic attack with a passage of Scripture, saying, "It is written . . . It is written . . . It is written . . ." After Jesus answered the tempter with Scripture, the Bible tells us that "the devil left him" (Matt. 4:11). So bathe your mind in Scripture passages that will armor plate your soul against the attacks of Satan—passages such as:

> I made a covenant with my eyes not to look lustfully at a girl (Job 31:1).

> Lead us not into temptation, but deliver us from the evil one (Matt. 6:13).

> Finally, brothers, whatever is true, whatever is noble, whatever is right, whatever is pure, whatever is lovely, whatever is admirable—if anything is excellent or praiseworthy—think about such things (Phil. 4:8).

> Marriage should be honored by all, and the marriage bed kept pure, for God will judge the adulterer and all the sexually immoral (Heb. 13:4).

Step 7: Put On the Armor of God

When tempted, you are on the battlefield of spiritual warfare, facing a cunning adversary. You can't pass the Test of Integrity unless you are armored against the enemy's attacks. As Paul writes:

> Put on the full armor of God so that you can take your stand against the devil's schemes. For our struggle is not against flesh

and blood, but against the rulers, against the authorities, against the powers of this dark world and against the spiritual forces of evil in the heavenly realms. Therefore put on the full armor of God, so that when the day of evil comes, you may be able to stand your ground, and after you have done everything, to stand. Stand firm then, with the belt of truth buckled around your waist, with the breastplate of righteousness in place, and with your feet fitted with the readiness that comes from the gospel of peace. In addition to all this, take up the shield of faith, with which you can extinguish all the flaming arrows of the evil one. Take the helmet of salvation and the sword of the Spirit, which is the word of God. And pray in the Spirit on all occasions with all kinds of prayers and requests. With this in mind, be alert and always keep on praying for all the saints (Eph. 6:11-18).

Let's look at each piece of the armor of God. First, there is the "belt of truth," which is your honesty and integrity. If you never compromise the truthfulness and wholeness of your character, you will never yield to temptation.

Second, there is the "breastplate of righteousness." Soldiers in Paul's day wore metal armor that protected the vital organs, especially the heart. The breastplate of righteousness armors your courage and your will. Satan will try to tear down your confidence in God. Don't let him. Trust the righteousness of God.

Third, Paul says you must have your "feet fitted with the readiness that comes from the gospel of peace." You are to wear the marching boots of the gospel. You are to be God's witnesses, spreading His gospel wherever you go. When you are busy taking the good news of Jesus Christ to other people, you won't have as much time on your hands to be tempted by sin.

Fourth, there is the "shield of faith, with which you can extinguish all the flaming arrows of the evil one." The soldiers of Paul's day used large wooden shields covered with leather to form a wall that couldn't be penetrated by the enemy's flaming arrows. Faith is your shield against Satan's fiery arrows. If you have trust in God and confidence in His power, you will be invulnerable to Satan's arrows of temptation.

Fifth, there is the "helmet of salvation." The helmet protects the head, which contains the brain. The helmet of salvation guards your thoughts. When you focus your thoughts on the salvation you have received through the cross of Christ, you are less likely to disgrace that salvation by yielding to lustful thoughts. Satan can't penetrate a mind that is focused on the wonder of salvation.

Sixth, there is the "sword of the Spirit, which is the word of God." The sword is an offensive weapon you wield to slay your enemy. When you quote Scripture to Satan, you wound him—and he runs from you. "Resist the devil, and he will flee from you" (Jas. 4:7). So read the Bible daily and memorize it so that you will always have the sword of the Spirit handy when you come under attack.

Judah failed the Integrity Test and brought disgrace upon himself. King David failed the Integrity Test, and it has been a stain on his reputation for 3,000 years. But Joseph passed the Integrity Test and achieved great things for God. May God give us the grace and strength to withstand the Integrity Test so that He can use us in mighty ways.

QUESTIONS FOR REFLECTION

1. Joseph resisted temptation and was punished with prison time. Have you ever been punished for doing the right thing? How did you feel?

2. If you can be punished by the world for your righteousness and godliness, why should you do the right thing? Why obey God if godliness gets you into trouble?

3. What was the worst sin Judah committed in the story of Judah and Tamar? What price did Judah pay for his sin?

4. Do you think everyone has a seal and staff like Judah—something of value that we put at risk when we sin? What do you possess that could be destroyed if you compromise your integrity? In other words, what do you possess that you would call your seal and staff?

5. What enemy do you fear the most: the world, the flesh or the devil? Explain your answer.

6. What changes can you make in your life right now to armor plate your soul against temptation?

Notes
1. John Eldredge, *Wild at Heart: Discovering the Secret of a Man's Soul* (Nashville, TN: Nelson Books, 2001), n.p.
2. Bruce Wilkinson, *Experiencing Spiritual Breakthroughs* (Sisters, OR: Multnomah, 1999), p. 111.
3. Ibid.

TEST NO. 3: THE PERSEVERANCE TEST

*You need to persevere so that when you have done the will of God,
you will receive what he has promised.*

HEBREWS 10:36

Although everyone knows of the J. C. Penney department store chain, few people know about the man who founded the company. James Cash Penney was born in 1875 on a farm near Hamilton, Missouri. He opened his first dry goods store in Kemmerer, Wyoming, in 1902.

Being a man of deep Christian faith and moral conviction, Penney named his store the "Golden Rule Store," after the guiding principle of his life. His store was so successful that within a decade he opened over 30 more Golden Rule Stores, ringing up sales of more than $2 million per year. From his earliest days in business, Penney tithed his income to the Lord. As his business and income grew, so did his giving. By the time of his death in 1971, Penney was giving 90 percent of his income to God.

J. C. Penney was amazingly successful over the course of his lifetime, yet he suffered many setbacks and was severely tested by adversity. His life is a testimony to the power of perseverance.

In 1910, Penney suffered a devastating loss when his wife died. He grieved deeply, relying on his faith and his work to see him through.

In 1913, he incorporated the J. C. Penney Company and phased out the Golden Rule name. He suffered a second devastating personal loss in 1923 when his second wife died while giving birth to his son. Again, he relied on God and his work to carry him through his sorrow.

By early 1929, there were 1,400 J. C. Penney department stores across the nation. The future seemed bright. Then in late October 1929, the stock market collapsed, precipitating the Great Depression. James Cash Penney lost $40 million in a single day. He had to sell almost all of his assets to pay his creditors. At age 54, Penney was flat broke.

The J. C. Penney stores continued to operate, but times were hard and the retail business was precarious. Penney suffered from anxiety and sleeplessness. His doctors prescribed tranquilizers, but the pills didn't help. He eventually became convinced that he was about to die. He checked into the Battle Creek Sanitarium in Battle Creek, Michigan, a holistic healing clinic founded by cereal magnate John Harvey Kellogg. One night, Penney wrote farewell letters to his family and friends, and then went to bed believing the end was near.

The next morning, he awoke to the sound of voices in the hospital chapel down the hall, singing this hymn:

> Be not dismayed whate'er betide,
> God will take care of you;
> Beneath His wings of love abide,
> God will take care of you.[1]

Penney left his room and went to the chapel. He sat in the back row and sang the hymn, and immediately he felt renewed in body and soul. Within days, he checked out of the sanitarium and returned home. With his faith and hope restored, Penney persevered through the adversity of the Great Depression and rebuilt his retail empire.

Looking back on this time in his life, James Cash Penney reflected, "It is a natural thing to want to succeed, but all are not willing to pay the price of success. Some folks have a wishbone instead of a backbone." J. C. Penney passed the Perseverance Test—the third of Joseph's four tests.

Joseph and the Perseverance Test

Joseph was 17 years old when he was sold into slavery. He was 30 years old when Pharaoh took him out of the prison and made him his second-in-command. That means that the time Joseph spent as a slave in Potiphar's house plus the time he spent in prison totaled 13 years. We don't know how many of those 13 years Joseph spent in prison, but some Bible scholars believe that it may have been as many as 12 years.

Imagine spending *12 years* in prison for a crime you didn't commit! Imagine spending *12 years* wondering why God was allowing you to suffer unjustly year after year. How would you feel toward God? Would it make you bitter? Would it make you lose hope? Or would you *persevere* in trusting God?

Remember also that Joseph had his hopes raised—and then dashed. When he correctly interpreted a dream for Pharaoh's cupbearer, Joseph asked the cupbearer to remember him and help him get out of prison. The Scriptures tell us, "The chief cupbearer, however, did not remember Joseph; he forgot him" (Gen. 40:23). How long did the cupbearer forget Joseph? Genesis 41 opens with these words: "When two full years had passed . . ."

Two years! Joseph languished in prison for two more years because he had been forgotten. "Hope deferred makes the heart sick," says Proverbs 13:12. Picture this heartsick young man in a dark, filthy, vermin-ridden prison, day after day, year after year. He had spent the end of his teenage years and the entire decade of his twenties in prison for a crime he didn't commit.

Many people under similar circumstances simply give up the fight and give up on God. Others try to hurry God's timetable or deliver themselves from their trial, but they only succeed in making matters worse. *It's a mistake to try to rush the work God is doing in our souls.*

During my seven-year Joseph Pit experience, I felt that I was walking a treadmill. I had to keep moving, but there was no destination in sight. I sank into depression every Monday morning, wondering how I was going to get through the week. My hope was deferred. My heart was sick.

But even though I wasn't aware of it at the time, God was working in my life. He was building my character. He was stripping away my pride.

He was preparing me for a new calling. Above all, He was teaching me to persevere.

Profiles in Perseverance

Novelist Irving Stone studied and fictionalized some of history's most fascinating lives. His novels include *Lust for Life* (the story of painter Vincent van Gogh), *Love Is Eternal* (based on the marriage of Abraham Lincoln and Mary Todd), and *The Agony and the Ecstasy* (the story of Michelangelo). Stone believed that all the great lives he wrote about had one common denominator: perseverance.

> I write about people who sometime in their life have a vision or dream of something that should be accomplished, and then they go to work. They are beaten over the head, knocked down, vilified and for years they get nowhere. But every time they're knocked down they stand up. You cannot destroy these people. And at the end of their lives they've accomplished some modest part of what they set out to do.[2]

When I think of someone who persevered in order to accomplish God's will for his life, I think of Cyrus McCormick. Born in 1809, Cyrus McCormick was an inventor who possessed the perseverance of Joseph. He was raised on a farm by his father, Robert Hall McCormick, who was also an inventor.

Cyrus McCormick sought to do what his father had tried and failed to do: invent a machine to harvest wheat. In 1831, at the age of 22, McCormick succeeded in building a working mechanical reaper. Three years later, he patented his invention. The future looked bright, but then, in 1837, a financial panic caused a run on the banks. McCormick lost his fortune and declared bankruptcy. In 1843, he suffered another setback when a legal loophole caused him to lose his patent. Suddenly, dozens of competitors began building and selling his mechanical reaper.

Although his share of the domestic market was shrinking, McCormick expanded into the European market in 1851. Five years later, his factories were producing more than 4,000 mechanical reapers per year.

McCormick used the profits to advance the gospel of Jesus Christ. He admired the evangelistic ministry of Dwight L. Moody, so in 1869 he donated $10,000 to help Moody start the Chicago YMCA. Before his death in 1884, McCormick also donated $100,000 to the Moody Bible Institute, which still educates students of the Bible today. Adversity produced perseverance in the life of Cyrus McCormick, and God used him to build the institutions that trained young Christians for service to Him.

Perseverance is the key to every great accomplishment because nothing of lasting value has ever been achieved without adversity. Industrialist Henry Ford is one of the great success stories of American history, but he failed in business five times before he succeeded. A Ford Motor Company employee once asked his boss the secret of success, and Henry Ford replied, "When you start a thing, don't quit until you finish it."

The path ahead of you is strewn with obstacles. People will oppose you. There will be financial setbacks, time pressures, illnesses and misfortunes. Some of the biggest obstacles will be inside of you: self-doubt, insecurity, procrastination, worry.

Perseverance, Paul says, is the virtue God uses to build our character in times of adversity: "And we rejoice in the hope of the glory of God. Not only so, but we also rejoice in our sufferings, because we know that suffering produces perseverance; perseverance, character; and character, hope" (Rom. 5:2-4). When we persevere through adversity, we win the approval of our Lord Jesus Christ, who told the suffering church at Ephesus, "I know your deeds, your hard work and your perseverance. . . . You have persevered and have endured hardships for my name, and have not grown weary" (Rev. 2:2-3). That, I'm sure, is the same commendation Joseph received from God when he passed the Perseverance Test.

Perseverance is a refusal to quit. It's falling down 100 times and getting back up 100 times. We need to remember that perseverance is not a matter of forcing doors to open; it's standing in front of the doors as long as it takes before God chooses to open them.

Life is a marathon, not a sprint. The race doesn't go to the swiftest, but to those who don't give up. We need endurance in order to deal with the stress of adversity. We must maintain a balanced diet, exercise regularly, and get plenty of rest. People give up or give out when they feel depleted—

when they physically, emotionally and spiritually run out of gas.

When going through adversity, watch out for pessimists, blamers and toxic personalities. Beware of people who try to talk you out of your dreams and goals. Spend time with optimists and encouragers. Seek out people of faith.

The Gibeonite Ruse

Watch out, too, for the Gibeonite Ruse—a trick of Satan that is intended to lure you off the path that God has planned for your life. The Gibeonite Ruse refers to the time when Joshua and the people of Israel were traveling through the Promised Land and came upon the Gibeonites (see Josh. 9). The Gibeonites had heard that Israel had destroyed the cities of Jericho and Ai, and they feared that they were next.

So the Gibeonites came up with a clever deception. They loaded up donkeys with worn-out sacks and wineskins. They put on worn, patched clothing and sandals. They took only bread that was dry and moldy. They made themselves appear to be travelers on a long trek. Then they approached Joshua and said, "We have come from a distant country; make a treaty with us."

At this point, Joshua made a major mistake. He failed to ask the counsel of the Lord. If he had gone before God in prayer, God would have told him that the Gibeonites were deceiving him. Because Joshua was fooled, he made a treaty with the Gibeonites.

This peace treaty was not pleasing to the Lord. Because Israel was deceived by the Gibeonite Ruse, the people of Israel had to take charge of the Gibeonites and make servants of them. Over time, many Israelites married Gibeonites, which introduced pagan customs to Israel.

The people of Israel paid a price for failing to persevere in the path God had planned for them. They were tricked by the Gibeonite Ruse. This is a trick that Satan still uses today to lure us off the path of God's will for our lives. If you have ever gone into a partnership or agreement with someone who doesn't share your faith, values, ethics and goals, you've been tricked by the Gibeonite Ruse.

The Gibeonite Ruse drains our emotional and spiritual energy. It eats up time and resources. That's what Joshua and the Israelites discovered thousands of years ago, and it's what many Christians continue to discover today.

The Gibeonite Ruse may take the form of a "get rich quick" scheme that promises to solve all of our problems and remove us from our trial of adversity. It might be a relationship that we think will meet our needs or cure our loneliness. But the Gibeonite Ruse causes us to settle for doing less than what God commanded us to do.

When God leads us through adversity, we need to endure it with patience and obedience. We should never take a shortcut through the valley of adversity, because it always ends up being the long way around. God always rewards patience; He always blesses obedience.

Obedience is the first step to victory over the circumstances of life. It's not enough to simply believe. We must live out our beliefs in obedience. When we obey, God moves on our behalf. The Israelites walked around Jericho seven times in obedience to God's command—and the walls fell. If the people had only walked around the city six times, God would not have acted. To be victorious, we have to obey and persevere.

Those like Joseph who pass the Perseverance Test will receive the crown of life. We have God's Word on it:

Blessed is the man who perseveres under trial, because when he has stood the test, he will receive the crown of life that God has promised to those who love him (Jas. 1:12).

Questions for Reflection

1. If God called you to spend a dozen years in prison, how would you respond? What would you do in order to persevere through such a trial of adversity?

2. Proverbs 13:12 tells us, "Hope deferred makes the heart sick." What are the delayed and deferred hopes in your life that make your heart sick? Does Joseph's story of deliverance bring hope to your heart? Why or why not?

3. What is the Perseverance Test that you are going through right now? Do you see any evidence that your trial of adversity is producing character and hope in your life?

4. Have you ever been tricked by the Gibeonite Ruse? Did you, like the Israelites, make the mistake of not consulting God? How did the Gibeonite Ruse hinder, delay or derail your life?

5. What is God's promise to you as you go through the Perseverance Test? How does God's promise encourage you as you undergo this time of testing in your life?

Notes

1. Civilla D. Martin, "God Will Take Care of You," first published in *Songs of Redemption and Praise,* 1905. http://www.cyberhymnal.org/htm/g/w/gwiltake.htm (accessed April 2006).
2. Irving Stone, quoted in Pat Williams and Jim Denney, *Go for the Magic* (Nashville, TN: Thomas Nelson, 1995), pp. 175-176.

TEST NO. 4: THE SUCCESS TEST

So Pharaoh said to Joseph, "I hereby put you in charge of the whole land of Egypt." Then Pharaoh took his signet ring from his finger and put it on Joseph's finger. He dressed him in robes of fine linen and put a gold chain around his neck.

GENESIS 41:41-42

Muhammad Ali is considered the greatest heavyweight boxer of all time. He won 56 of his 61 professional fights and knocked out 37 opponents. His most famous catchphrase was, "I am the greatest!"

One day, Ali was seated in an airplane when the flight attendant came up the aisle to make sure that all the passengers had their seatbelts fastened. Reaching Ali's seat, she asked him to buckle up.

"Hmph!" the champ sneered. "Superman don't need no seatbelt!"

The flight attendant smiled sweetly and replied, "Superman don't need no airplane, either."

Ali fastened his seatbelt.

The greater our success, the greater the risk of us thinking too highly of ourselves. The fourth and final test Joseph faced was probably the most dangerous test of all: the Success Test.

Tested in the Crucible

At the end of my seven-year Joseph Pit experience, God caused my business to prosper and healed my broken finances. After years of struggle,

I should have been ecstatic to experience financial blessing once more. Instead, I discovered that material success just didn't mean as much as it once did. I had learned to live with adversity, and I was satisfied that I could live that way for the rest of my life if God called me to do so.

I had finally "died." I was dead to pride, dead to worldly wants and desires, dead to the drive for status and achievement, dead to ambition. Only when I was finally dead to all of those things could I truly be alive to Christ. As Paul tells us, "We were therefore buried with him through baptism into death in order that, just as Christ was raised from the dead through the glory of the Father, we too may live a new life" (Rom. 6:4). After my seven-year trial had burned the old life out of me, God gave me a new one.

How can you tell when your trial will be over? I believe your trial will end when it doesn't matter anymore. It will end when you have put your trust so completely in God that pressures, problems and material things no longer have a hold on you. It will end when your pride and worldliness have been scorched out of your soul.

When Joseph was elevated to his high position, he took the reins of leadership without becoming egotistical and self-important. Whether he was in Pharaoh's deepest dungeon or in Pharaoh's highest throne room, Joseph was the same man. He remained God's obedient servant regardless of his circumstances. Why? Because he had learned to be humble and content in all situations. Where had he acquired this rare character quality? He acquired it during his trial of adversity.

After 13 years as a slave and a prisoner, I believe that Joseph discovered the same thing I did after my seven-year Joseph Pit experience: Once you've lived a long time in a state of adversity, status and influence don't mean very much anymore. You appreciate the blessings God gives you, but if they were removed, you'd still be okay. Your security is in God, not circumstances.

Bible teacher R. T. Kendall offers this assessment of Joseph's spiritual and emotional state:

Joseph's day of exaltation had arrived. . . . He watched as the Pharaoh took his ring off his finger and put it on Joseph's finger.

Joseph never asked for that. All he wanted was to go home. . . . But a one-way ticket to Canaan wasn't available. Before he knew it, he had Egypt in his hip pocket. He had never prayed for that. But God wanted Egypt. What God wanted is what Joseph got. Joseph was given something that he could be trusted with because it didn't mean that much to him.[1]

How did Joseph reach the point where God could trust him with the fate of a nation? He reached that point by going through a series of tests. Proverbs 17:3 tells us, "The crucible for silver and the furnace for gold, but the LORD tests the heart." The leaders who have made the greatest mark for the kingdom of God have always had to pass through the crucible of adversity.

God knows that the human heart is filled with flaws and impurities. So He lovingly places us in the crucible of adversity to refine us and purify us. The greater the responsibility He intends for us, the hotter the crucible of preparation.

The Danger of Success

Scottish historian Thomas Carlyle observed, "Adversity is sometimes hard upon a man; but for one man who can stand prosperity there are a hundred that will stand adversity." And Oswald Chambers wrote, "Sudden elevation frequently leads to pride and a fall. The most exacting test of all to survive is prosperity."

Joseph passed the Success Test. At Pharaoh's side, he managed the affairs of Egypt with wisdom, grace and compassion. He ruled by serving and served by ruling. When Joseph passed the Success Test, he became an example to each of us of what authentic leadership is all about.

There is another biblical leader whose example is worth studying. He started well by serving God humbly and obediently. But near the end of his story, he failed the Success Test. His name was Gideon.

The story of Gideon is found in Judges 6 through 8. Israel was at war with the Midianites and the Amalekites. So God chose a humble young man, Gideon, to lead Israel and cleanse the land of idols. Gideon requested proof that this command came from God. He placed a wool fleece on the ground overnight, and the Lord caused the fleece to be wet with dew while the ground remained dry.

Gideon obeyed the Lord and destroyed the pagan idols in the region. Then he summoned a large army—over 30,000 men—to fight the Midianites and Amalekites. God said the army was too large, so He first reduced Gideon's army to 10,000 men, and then to a mere 300 men. When God gave Israel the victory with an army of only 300 men, all of Israel knew that it was the power of God, not military might, that had won the battle. After Israel's victory, the people asked Gideon to be their king, but Gideon told them that God alone should be their king.

If the story had ended there, all would have been well. But at the moment of Israel's triumph, Gideon stumbled. He told the people, "I do have one request, that each of you give me an earring from your share of the plunder." The Israelites took the gold from the bodies of the enemy dead and Gideon melted it and fashioned it into an idol. The Bible calls this idol an *ephod*, a word that refers to a ceremonial breast-plate—Gideon probably depicted the Lord God as a warrior with an ephod of gold.

But God does not allow Himself to be represented by an idol. This idol was an offense against God and a trap for the people. "All Israel prostituted themselves by worshiping [the idol] there, and it became a snare to Gideon and his family" (Judg. 8:27). After Gideon's death, the Israelites again worshiped the pagan god Baal. They forgot the Lord God who rescued them from their enemies.

The story of Gideon has a great beginning, but a tragic ending. This is an instructive lesson for us all. As the apostle Paul tells us, "If you think you are standing firm, be careful that you don't fall!" (1 Cor. 10:12).

What should we do if we fail the Success Test? Go back to God without fear. We can ask Him to help us learn the lessons of our failure and to strengthen us for another effort. The God of second chances is able to accomplish His purpose through us even if we have failed Him many times before.

Keys to Passing the Success Test

Here are five principles to remember when we graduate from a time of adversity to a time of blessing. If we keep these principles in mind, we will pass the Success Test—and God will use us in mighty ways.

1. View Success as a Gift from God

First, learn to see all of your successes as a gift from God, not as your own achievement. "But remember the LORD your God, for it is he who gives you the ability to produce wealth, and so confirms his covenant, which he swore to your forefathers, as it is today" (Deut. 8:18).

In Daniel, there is a scene in which the king of Babylon, Nebuchadnezzar, is walking on the roof of his palace. He says, "Is not this the great Babylon I have built as the royal residence, by my mighty power and for the glory of my majesty?" In answer, a voice from heaven says, "Your royal authority has been taken from you. You will be driven away from people and will live with the wild animals; you will eat grass like cattle." So the king became a madman for seven years. God humbled him so that he would learn to acknowledge his blessings as a gift from God (see Dan. 4:29-34).

The Lord is the source of all success, all elevation, all blessing. If you have a good mind and a healthy body, if you live in a land of opportunity, if you have a good education, if you've been given a few breaks, then you have much to be grateful for—and no cause for arrogance. You didn't *achieve* success; you *received* it as a gift.

"What makes you better than anyone else?" asks the apostle Paul. "What do you have that God hasn't given you? And if all you have is from God, why boast as though you have accomplished something on your own?" (1 Cor. 4:7, *NLT*). Name one thing you possess that is not a gift from God. The food you eat? The roof over your head? Your business? Your family? Your friends? Your relationship with God? It's all a gift, my friend. You may have worked hard for it, but even your ability to work is a gift! When all you have is a gift, there's no room for pride—only humility and gratitude.

2. Learn How to Handle Praise

If someone gushes over your accomplishments, accept it, but don't let it go to your head. Avoid the extremes of false modesty ("Don't praise me—

I'm no good.") and egotism ("Yeah, I'm really awesome!"). If someone praises you, just say, "Thank you," and move on.

The only praise we should seek is praise from our Lord: "Well done, good and faithful servant." The approval of people comes and goes, but the approval of God lasts forever. When you try to win praise, you are stealing from God. All praise belongs to Him.

3. Live a Humble Life

You need to voluntarily humble yourself before God—or God will have to humble you Himself. You must view yourself realistically. You should not have an inflated opinion of yourself, nor a deflated self-image. Paul writes:

> For by the grace given me I say to every one of you: Do not think of yourself more highly than you ought, but rather think of yourself with sober judgment, in accordance with the measure of faith God has given you (Rom. 12:3).

People often compliment me on how the *TGIF* devotionals I write bless their lives. I know it is only through God's grace that I am able to write them. I also know that if I think more highly of myself than I should, God will send a reproof in my life to judge the pride in me.

Some people think that humility means constantly disparaging and demeaning themselves. But there's nothing humble about saying, "I'm such a worm! I'm a worthless sinner! I can't do anything right!" That may sound oh-so-humble, but constant self-deprecation is actually a self-centered form of thinking. After all, every one of those sentences begins with "I"! As Rick Warren observes in *The Purpose-Driven Life*, "Humility is not thinking less of yourself, it's thinking of yourself less."[2]

The apostle Peter writes, "All of you, clothe yourselves with humility toward one another, because, 'God opposes the proud but gives grace to the humble.' Humble yourselves, therefore, under God's mighty hand, that he may lift you up in due time" (1 Pet. 5:5-6). If we lift ourselves up in pride and arrogance, God will humble us. But if we humble ourselves under God's mighty hand, He will lift us up.

4. Be Held Accountable for Humility

Ask people to hold you accountable for a humble attitude. Invite a few close, trusted friends and family members to observe your behavior in the workplace, at church and at home. Tell them, "If you see that I'm acting more like a boss than a servant—if you see any sign of success going to my head—you have my permission to bring me up short and put me in my place. The goal of my life is to become more like Christ, and I'm counting on you to keep me focused on that goal."

A close friend once accused me of self-promotion in my ministry. I had to evaluate whether his comment had merit, so I took his comments to my wife, employees and advisory board. My advisors concluded that while our organization's attitude remained humble, some of our marketing approaches might give a boastful impression. So we modified our activities in light of my friend's comment. True humility accepts constructive criticism with an open mind.

5. Remember That God Saved You and Has Plans for You

We need to remember to focus on the amazing fact that God saved us and wants to use us for His plans and purposes. The very fact that Jesus Christ died to save us is humbling. God didn't have to send His Son to die in our place. In truth, we deserve nothing but everlasting punishment. Every good thing that happens in our lives is a blessing of God's grace far beyond our deserving.

Not only has God saved us from our sin, but He also has actually chosen to accomplish His eternal plan through us, flawed and fallible as we are. God may place a Joseph Calling on our lives because He has sovereignly chosen to use us as instruments of His perfect will. Unbelievable! I identify with the apostle Paul when he marvels, "I thank Christ Jesus our Lord . . . that he considered me faithful, appointing me to his service" (1 Tim. 1:12).

If God in His wisdom and mercy should choose to elevate us to a high position in the business world, in the entertainment world, in government, in the military, or in the church, we should pray for the grace to be humble. We should daily fall on our faces, giving Him all the glory, because we deserve no glory for ourselves.

Remember Why God Blessed You

When David became king after the death of King Saul, he went from one victory to the next. He gathered a great army of mighty men. With those men, he won battles against the Philistines and seized the city of Jerusalem from the Jebusites. Moving his capital from Hebron to Jerusalem, David took up residence in the fortress. The Scriptures tell us that "David became more and more powerful, because the LORD Almighty was with him" (1 Chron. 11:9).

A little later, we find an instructive statement about King David's attitude: "And David knew that the LORD had established him as king over Israel and that his kingdom had been highly exalted for the sake of his people Israel" (1 Chron. 14:2). Early in his career, King David understood that God had blessed him for the sake of Israel, not for his own benefit.

Years later, King David would tragically lose sight of this all-important truth, and his arrogance would lead him into adultery, murder and shame. That's why it's important to continually maintain our humility before God.

The Lord once said, "I have found David son of Jesse a man after my own heart" (Acts 13:22). If a man like David can succumb to pride and sin, it can happen to any of us. We must always remember that God never blesses us for our exclusive benefit; He calls us to be a blessing to others.

Robert "R. G." LeTourneau was an inventor and manufacturer of large earthmoving equipment. When the Allies landed in France on D-Day, June 6, 1944, most of the large machinery used in the invasion was designed and built by LeTourneau. LeTourneau was a devoted Christian and founder of LeTourneau University in Longview, Texas.

LeTourneau's early years as a Christian were filled with adversity. At age 14, he was a high school dropout who shoveled sand at an iron factory in Oregon. By his late twenties, he had worked at nearly 40 different jobs, he and his wife had lost a child in infancy, and he had broken his neck in a car crash. He was 31 when his Stockton, California, repair shop failed, leaving him $5,000 in debt. LeTourneau would have filed for bankruptcy if a kindhearted banker hadn't given him a loan, asking for no collateral.

LeTourneau started a new business that manufactured heavy equipment—and finally found his calling. For a while, he wondered if he was truly walking in God's will by being a businessman instead of a preacher. He took his doubts to his pastor, who said, "Brother LeTourneau, God needs Christian businessmen as much as He needs preachers and missionaries."

Over the years, LeTourneau's company kept building bigger earthmoving machines—and making bigger profits. Through those years, R. G. LeTourneau committed his business and finances to the Lord. He contributed sacrificially to missionary work in Africa and South America. Near the end of his career, he gave 90 percent of his income to God and lived on the remaining 10 percent. He once said, "The question is not how much of my money I give to God, but rather how much of God's money I keep for myself."

Are you prepared for what God wants to do with your life? Are you prepared for Him to promote you to the next level? Once you have passed the first three tests of adversity, make sure you are ready for the hardest test of all—the Success Test.

QUESTIONS FOR REFLECTION

1. What does it mean to die to pride, to worldly wants and desires, and to ambition? Is it a sin to be ambitious? Why or why not?

2. How does the fact that God lovingly places you in the crucible of adversity to refine, purify, shape and form your life make you feel toward God? Does it make you love Him more? Does it make you fear Him? Explain your answer.

3. Are you ready to handle success and elevation? Explain your answer.

4. In this chapter, we see that both Gideon and King David showed great faith and accomplished great deeds for God and His people. Yet both also fell into tragic error later in their lives. What lessons do you see in the lives of Gideon and David?

5. Is it easy or hard for you to be humble? What is one step you can take to build a deeper quality of humility into your character? How can your Christian friends help you in that regard?

6. How would you define stewardship? If you are a steward of all that you have, then who is the owner? What steps have you taken to be a good steward of the time, talent, ideas, money and other resources God has entrusted to you? What additional steps do you need to take to be an even better steward?

Notes
1. R. T. Kendall, *A Treasury of Wisdom Journal* (Uhrichsville, OH: Barbour and Company, 1996), January 16 reading.
2. Rick Warren, *The Purpose-Driven Life* (Grand Rapids, MI: Zondervan Publishing House, 2002), p. 148.

PART III

WHY WE SUFFER

WHY DO GOOD PEOPLE SUFFER?

But even if you should suffer for what is right, you are blessed.

1 PETER 3:14

Grace Parker (not her real name) was born to a poor family in rural Georgia. When she was an infant, her alcoholic father asked her mother for a divorce. His reason: He had just gotten a teenage girl pregnant. When Grace's mother refused, he flew into a rage, grabbed Grace and threw her across the room, and then began strangling Grace's mother.

Just then, Grace's grandfather came into the room and saved Grace's mother from being murdered. Grace's father, a Marine, fled to the military base and told his commanding officer what he had done. The local police couldn't touch him, because he was under military jurisdiction. The next day, he shipped out to Hawaii.

Although Grace was miraculously uninjured from being tossed across the room, she was diagnosed with polio at age one. The doctors said that she would never walk. Without any income, Grace's mother moved into a government housing project. Grace and her mother rarely had enough to eat. Most of their meals consisted of potatoes.

On one occasion, Grace and her mother had not had anything to eat in days, so Grace's mother went to her knees and cried out, "O God, just send us some food and I'll follow You the rest of my life!" The next morning, her mother opened the front door and found the porch lined from end to end with bags of groceries. After that, Grace's mother began attending church.

When Grace's mother found work, her greatest challenge was finding childcare for Grace. One Sunday at church, a Christian woman noticed Grace's physical condition and offered to care for her at no charge. Every weekday for a year, this woman cared for Grace in her home, laid hands on her, and prayed for her healing. One day while she was carrying Grace in her arms, the woman fell down the stairs. Grace was unhurt, but the woman suffered a broken hip.

The day after the fall, Grace's mother was putting the child's leg braces on—and was shocked to discover that the girl's toes were wiggling. Within a week, Grace learned to walk on her own. The Lord had miraculously healed her.

Suffering Innocence

Grace was four when her father returned home. His alcoholism had worsened, and he began beating Grace and sexually molesting her. He did everything he could to destroy her self-esteem.

Once when Grace was five, her infant sister was crying. Grace tried to pick the baby up and comfort her, but she tripped and dropped the baby. Her parents picked up the unconscious baby and the whole family rushed to the hospital. Arriving at the emergency room entrance, Grace's mother whisked the baby into the hospital. Grace and her dad stayed in the car. He turned a hateful glare on Grace and said, "If that baby dies, I'll kill you!"

Grace dropped to her knees and prayed, "God, please let my sister live so that I can live!" Instantly, she felt God's comforting presence. For the first time in her life, she knew that God cared about her. Knowing that God was with her sustained her through the horrors of her childhood.

God provided food for the family through the local pool hall. Each night, Grace's mother would ride her bicycle to the pool hall and wait outside. Some nights, the owner would give her some leftover chili before they washed up the pots. Grace and her sisters would watch through the window for their mother's return, hoping to see a sack hanging on the bicycle handlebars.

When Grace was seven, her father crashed the family car, injuring himself and two of Grace's siblings. After the accident, a local church brought groceries to the family. That display of Christian generosity made a big impact on Grace. She told God that when she grew up, she wanted to help boys and girls who were poor and hungry.

At school, Grace wore ragged clothes sewn from old window curtains. Although the other children ostracized her, Grace had an intimate relationship with God. Her teachers were constantly amazed at her joyful attitude.

At 18, Grace fell in love with a Christian man who accepted her unconditionally. There were problems in their relationship because of the sexual abuse in her past, but God gradually healed her memories. She later married this young man.

Today Grace says, "You can choose to be the victim of your circumstances or you can take a baby step toward the Father. Often, we get so busy trying to fix ourselves that we forget the One who holds every tiny detail in His hands. We forget to sit in His lap and say, 'Daddy, I need You. I need Your help!' I experienced a Father who does not give us a stone when we ask for bread. Instead, He offers extravagant love to His children and a place to feel safe when we feel surrounded by danger. There's no one like Him!"

Grace is now involved in a ministry to the poor and serves on staff with a ministry that encourages people to become intercessors and prayer warriors. She is living proof that we do not have to remain victims of the past. God works through our worst adversity and uses our pain to prepare us for a lifetime of ministry.

But Grace's story also confronts us with a difficult and troubling question: Why does God allow good people to suffer?

The Shadow of His Hand

"Whenever God gives a vision to a saint," wrote Oswald Chambers, "He puts him, as it were, in the shadow of His hand, and the saint's duty is to be still and listen."[1] We see this principle in Genesis 15 when God makes His covenant with Abraham (who was then called Abram).

As the story begins, the word of the Lord comes to Abram in a vision: "Do not be afraid, Abram. I am your shield, your very great reward." Although Abram trusts God, he questions God and asks how He can keep His promise of making him a great nation, since he has no children. God does not explain how His promise will be fulfilled. He simply says, "Look up at the heavens and count the stars—if indeed you can count them. So shall your offspring be."

Abram believes God, and God makes a covenant with him involving the sacrifice of several animals. The sacrifices symbolize the coming sacrifice of Jesus the Messiah. After Abram makes the sacrifices, the sun begins to set and Abram falls into a deep sleep. Genesis 15:12 says, "a thick and dreadful darkness came over" Abram. It is in the depths of that strange and terrible darkness that God tells Abram that his descendents will one day be slaves in a strange country, but they will come out of that nation with great possessions and return to the land that we now call the Holy Land.

The darkness that covered Abram, though it seemed thick and dreadful, was, in fact, the darkness of God's hand of blessing and promise. While Abram was in this shadow of darkness, he received the promise of a homeland for his descendents. That homeland—Israel—is the dwelling place of Abraham's descendents to this very day.

Abraham had to go through a thick and dreadful darkness in order to hear God's promise of future blessing. Joseph had to go through the darkness of adversity for 13 years in order to fulfill God's promise that Abraham's descendents would live in a strange country, Egypt. Years later, Moses had to go through the darkness of the desert of Midian to fulfill God's promise that Abraham's descendents would come out of Egypt.

This is always the pattern: We must first go through darkness before we are able to receive the light of God's promise. From our limited perspective, the darkness seems evil and threatening. But from the perspective of Scripture, the darkness is the shadow of God's hand.

In many segments of the Church today, people are wrongly taught that the darkness of adversity is a sign that God has removed His blessing.

Some teach that if we go through trials, God must be punishing the sin in our life. This is the same false teaching for which God rebuked Job's three "miserable comforters." The Scriptures teach us that trials are a normal part of our walk with God. Before Jesus went through the darkness of the cross, He told His followers, "In this world you will have trouble. But take heart! I have overcome the world" (John 16:33).

Sometimes, God must take us through the darkness to shape our character so that we can be conformed to the image of His Son, Jesus. Paul, in his letter to the Christians suffering persecution in Rome, said, "For those God foreknew he also predestined to be conformed to the likeness of his Son, that he might be the firstborn among many brothers" (Rom. 8:29).

At other times, God takes us through darkness so that we can learn what it means to identify with the sufferings of Christ. As Paul writes, "I want to know Christ and the power of his resurrection and the fellowship of sharing in his sufferings, becoming like him in his death" (Phil. 3:10). And Peter agrees: "But rejoice that you participate in the sufferings of Christ, so that you may be overjoyed when his glory is revealed" (1 Pet. 4:13).

God sometimes takes us through the darkness to prepare us for the amazing ministry He has planned for us. If we never experience mistreatment, opposition or suffering of our own, we might never understand the hurts of others. As the apostle Paul puts it:

Praise be to the God and Father of our Lord Jesus Christ, the Father of compassion and the God of all comfort, who comforts us in all our troubles, so that we can comfort those in any trouble with the comfort we ourselves have received from God. For just as the sufferings of Christ flow over into our lives, so also through Christ our comfort overflows (2 Cor. 1:3-5).

In the first two years of my trial of adversity, I had many questions. I questioned the love of God. I questioned my own belief system. As the walls closed in on me, my questions became urgent cries demanding an answer. Again and again, I raised questions as old as the book of Job:

"God, if You are loving, just and all-powerful, why do You allow good people to suffer?" Evangelist Billy Graham addressed this question in his book *Answers to Life's Problems*:

> We do not know all the reasons why God permits evil. We need to remember, however, that he is not the cause of evil in this world and we should therefore not blame Him for it. Remember that God did not create evil, as some believe. God created the world perfect. Man chose to defy God and go his own way, and it is man's fault that evil entered the world. Even so, God has provided the ultimate triumph of good over evil in Jesus Christ, who on the cross, defeated Satan and those who follow him. Christ is coming back and when He does, all evil will be ended forever and righteousness and justice will prevail.
>
> Have you ever thought about what would happen if God suddenly eliminated all the evil in this world? Not one person would be left, because we are all guilty of sin. "If you, O Lord, kept a record of sins, O Lord, who could stand?" (Psalm 130:3). As the Bible says, "Because of the Lord's great love we are not consumed, for his compassions never fail" (Lamentations 3:22).[2]

Sometimes we demand to know if the adversity we are facing in our life is from God or from Satan. The truth is that it really doesn't matter. All that matters is that nothing happens without God's permission. All the events in our lives are filtered through His will for our lives. True, we can open ourselves up to adversity by rebelling against God's commands. But many times, the adversity we experience has nothing to do with sin on our part. It's simply part of the Joseph Calling that God has placed on our lives.

Whenever we suffer, we should remember that the Son of God went before us, drinking the cup of suffering and death to the dregs. Because Christ is fully man and fully God, we know that God understands our fears, sorrows and suffering. He identifies with us. Most important of all, the Father has given us the gift of His Son so that we don't have to die and suffer forever in eternity. Because Jesus suffered and died for us, our suffering can be made like His—purposeful and meaningful.

Evil, suffering and death came into the world when the first man and woman listened to Satan and committed the first sin. Evil was never part of the Garden of Eden. The moment Adam and Eve crossed the boundary of God's command, evil became the terrible reality of this world. As Bill Johnson writes in *When Heaven Invades Earth*:

> Satan didn't come into the Garden violently and take possession of Adam and Eve. He couldn't. Why? He had no dominion there. Dominion empowers. And since man was given the keys of dominion over the planet, the devil would have to get his authority from them. The suggestion to eat the forbidden fruit was simply the devil's effort to get Adam and Eve to agree with him in opposition to God, thus empowering him. Through that agreement he is enabled to kill, steal, and destroy. It's important to realize that even today Satan is empowered through man's agreement.[3]

In times of suffering, only one thing matters: clinging by faith to the God who loves us. One day in eternity, Jesus will wipe away all our tears and answer all our questions.

You Are Not Entitled

Brett Rademacher became a Christian at age 19, but he was never able to connect his faith with his work. He was in his mid-thirties when, through a series of events and revelations, God led him into the network marketing industry—an industry of which he didn't originally have a high opinion. He experienced some success as a distributor for several different companies, but his success was always short-lived, as those companies went out of business.

One day, Brett received a copy of *God@Work* by Rich Marshall. To this day, Brett has no idea who sent him the book. Reading that book was a life-changing experience that transformed Brett's understanding of the higher calling that God had for his life. Shortly after reading the book, God told Brett that he should be anointed with oil. "It was very clear," Brett later told me. "God spoke it right into my spirit. I have never experienced anything like it since—and it changed my whole reality of God."

Brett obeyed God, went to church, and was anointed with oil for his business. Almost immediately, the network marketing company he was involved with experienced a surge in sales and profits. Within two and a half years, he was earning more than $500,000 per month from his various network-marketing endeavors and was considered one of the top Internet-based network marketers in the world.

One day, Brett received a prophetic word from a Christian woman that he met in Hawaii. She told him that a time was coming when he would be abased. The woman told him that this would take place according to God's plan, and that he shouldn't fight it or it would take longer.

Two months later, Brett's sales empire came crashing down when the Federal Trade Commission filed suit against him, claiming that the product he sold didn't do what the manufacturers claimed. Brett didn't make the product—he just sold it—but he had always believed in it. The Federal Trade Commission named him in the suit because of the significant commissions he earned. They assumed he was an owner in the company that manufactured the product.

The legal action against Brett was expensive and emotionally devastating. He suffered from deep depression. He recalled, "I wondered why God would tell me to get anointed and bless my business—and then pull the plug!" Unable to sell the product that was his mainstay, Brett had to lay off most of his staff, including many close friends. In time, he was forced to shut down his marketing company.

A longtime *TGIF* subscriber, Brett called and asked for my help. I met him in Lake Tahoe and, over a three-hour lunch, he confided to me some of his struggles in the multilevel marketing industry. He said that he'd often been lied to and exploited by others in the business. The Holy Spirit prompted me to say, "That's because the ruling spirit in this industry is greed and deceit. I believe that God has called you to play a part in cleaning up the multilevel marketing industry."

"But how?" he said. "I've got a federal lawsuit on my back. I'm being driven out of business."

"Brett," I said, "do you know what circumcision is?"

This question surprised him. "Well, I know what circumcision is, but what does that have to do with the trouble I'm facing?"

"In Joshua 5, there's a scene in which the men of Israel, on entering the Promised Land, must undergo circumcision. The removal of their foreskins represented a break with the past. They became new people. When we undergo circumcision, we shed the former things. Once the former life has been discarded, God pronounces His blessing. You're going through a time of circumcision because God is preparing you for the Promised Land."

"Wow!" Brett said. "I've been feeling that I was being punished by God—and I didn't know why! I always felt that if I did all the right things, I was entitled to prosperity!"

"Unfortunately, that's the theology most of us learn in church," I said.

Eventually, the United States District Court entered a stipulated final judgment without going to trial. In the judgment, Brett was found not liable for any of the wrongdoing the Federal Trade Commission had alleged. Even so, Brett was required to pay $500,000, though it was stated that the money was not a fine or penalty. Looking back, Brett realizes that everything he went through—the anointing, the phenomenal success and the disastrous crash—were all divinely appointed events. God was doing a powerful work *within* his life so that He could later do a powerful work *through* his life.

Recently, God called Brett back into the network marketing industry after an 18-month hiatus. Brett now has a renewed sense of what it means to live out his faith in the workplace.

I find that most Christians today believe as Brett once did: If they do all the right things, God *owes* them a life of blessing, good health, happiness and prosperity. I operated under the same assumption before my Joseph Pit experience. I thought that because of my faithfulness, God owed me a good marriage and a successful business. That's a false assumption—an attitude of entitlement. We're not entitled to a thing from God. *Obedience can't be viewed as an insurance policy against adversity. Every blessing we receive is a gift of His grace.*

Once we realize that God doesn't owe us anything, we gain a new perspective on the question, Why do good people suffer? We realize that we are not entitled to a trouble-free life.

Getting Outside of Your Pain

Nan Jarvis was born into a family of nine children. Her father committed suicide when she was three. During her childhood in South Africa, she was sexually molested by her uncles. When she reached adulthood, she married an abusive man who beat her and sexually abused her throughout their three-year marriage. Finally, she filed for divorce and moved with her son, Richard, to the nearby nation of Swaziland on the southeast tip of Africa.

During Nan's long trial of adversity, she yielded her life to Jesus Christ. Soon after committing herself to Christ, Nan sensed that God had a purpose for her suffering. She saw the suffering of the Swazi people and began looking for ways to demonstrate God's love to the people around her.

Swaziland, a nation of one million people, leads the world in the number of HIV/AIDS cases per capita. *Thirty-nine percent* of the population is infected with the virus that causes AIDS. More than a third of the population is unemployed, and most of Swaziland's people live on less than a dollar per day. The people of Swaziland are held in the grip of witchcraft, ancestor worship, sexual immorality and polygamy. Meanwhile, Swaziland's king, Mswati III, has been criticized for spending millions on limousines, a luxury jet and mansions for his 13 wives.[4]

Nan opened a flower shop in one of Swaziland's two capital cities. Her original plan was to have her staff make the deliveries while she remained in the shop and supervised the floral arrangements. However, soon after Nan opened her business, she felt the Holy Spirit prompting her to make all of the deliveries herself. This opened doors for her to go into homes, hospitals, clinics, government offices and even the king's palaces. There, God gave her opportunities to share the gospel, pray with people, and witness His healing in many people's lives.

One of Nan's most surprising opportunities came when she picked up an account for King Mswati himself. The king commissioned her to deliver fresh flowers on a regular basis to the mansions of his queens. Over time, Nan developed a friendship with many of the king's wives.

One of the wives, Queen LaMbikiza, gave her life to the Lord and received the power of the Holy Spirit. She has since shared her faith and has had an influence for Christ within the palace and around the country. Queen LaMbikiza has become a controversial figure in the nation by earning a law degree and practicing law in the Swazi high court. But the queen is convinced that she's following God's will and serving her people as an advocate of the law. She also promotes gospel music in Swaziland through a choir she organized. The queen has influenced King Mswati to make important reforms to alleviate poverty, ignorance and AIDS in the country.

Nan Jarvis's relationship with the people of Swaziland opened doors for her to bring agricultural programs to the nation through the International Christian Chamber of Commerce and other groups. She has prayed and seen God send rain for the crops of Swaziland. She says God has told her that Swaziland will become a "bread basket nation" that will feed itself and other nations.

After years of abuse and mistreatment during her long Joseph Pit experience, God elevated Nan Jarvis to a place of ministry and leadership in her adopted country. She is living proof that God still weaves our pain and brokenness into ministry for a nation, just as He did in Joseph's day. Although she suffered incredible mistreatment in the past, Nan chooses to focus on the needs of others, not on her own hurts. Her example shows us that *the best way to get beyond our pain is to get outside of ourselves and focus on others.* The more we help others, the more we help ourselves.

A 1988 article in *Psychology Today* reported on an experiment involving 1,700 women under stress. The women participated in various projects that involved helping other people. Within 30 days, 85 percent of the women reported that they had been relieved of stress symptoms that included "stress-related disorders such as headaches, voice loss and even pain accompanying lupus and multiple sclerosis."[5]

I suspect that many people could save thousands of dollars on therapy and antidepressants if they would just take time to serve others. The best way to get *beyond* our pain is to get *outside* of it.

The Suffering of Job

The question of why good people suffer is a central theme of the book of Job. The first verse of the book of Job describes Job as "blameless and upright," a man who "feared God and shunned evil." Although Job was a godly man, God allowed him to suffer horrible loss and pain—yet Job remained loyal and faithful to God. Even so, he had many questions. It's significant to note that God never answered Job's questions. In the end, Job had to take a great deal on faith alone—and so do we.

The theme "Why do we suffer?" is introduced in the first chapter of Job. After God allows Satan to attack Job's possessions and his family, Job loses his herds, his wealth, and even his 10 beloved children. Later, Job also loses his health. All of this happens to a man God calls "blameless and upright"!

Despite his suffering, Job maintains his trust in God. When his wife tells him to curse God and drop dead, Job replies, "You are talking like a foolish woman. Shall we accept good from God, and not trouble?" And the Bible adds, "In all this, Job did not sin in what he said" (Job 2:10).

Soon, three of Job's friends hear of his suffering and come to comfort him. Before long, however, they start arguing and accusing him of sin. They basically say to Job, "God is just and fair and would never cause anyone to suffer unjustly. Therefore, if you are suffering, you must deserve it." Sounds logical, but the world doesn't work that way. Joseph was a godly man, yet he suffered. So there must be a reason why bad things happen to godly people. And there is.

From the beginning of the book of Job, we see that Job suffers because Satan has rebelled against God. After Satan rebelled, he tempted human beings—Adam and Eve—to join him in sinning against God. Ever since Adam and Eve fell, humans have lived in a universe at war. As long as that rebellion continues, injustice and sin will be rampant throughout the world, because the god of this world is Satan.

However, even though Satan challenges God's authority over His creation, God is still sovereign over all. Nothing happens in the universe without His permission. When bad things happen to God's people, He turns bad things into His good. The apostle Paul puts it this way: "And we know that in all things God works for the good of those who love him, who have been called according to his purpose" (Rom. 8:28). In other words, when God calls us to serve His eternal purpose, He weaves the affliction, sorrow and pain of our lives into something of eternal value.

The book of Job points out another important perspective on why good people suffer—a perspective that most of us entirely miss. Part of the problem with asking the question, Why do good people suffer? is that it assumes the world is divided into good people and bad people. The fact is that no one is truly good. Even though God described Job as blameless and upright, Job was not sinless. He was a fallen man. As the psalmist observes, "There is no one who does good, not even one" (Ps. 53:3). Not even Job!

As we read through the book of Job, we see that Job does not have this perspective. He thinks that God has made some sort of mistake in allowing him to suffer. He thinks that if he could only make God understand that he's innocent, the Lord would take away his affliction.

But beginning in Job 38 and continuing for three straight chapters, God responds by asking Job question after question. In essence, God demands to know, "Can you create anything from nothing, Job? Is your wisdom equal to Mine?" In the end, Job is ashamed for having brought up the subject. He confesses that God is incapable of making a mistake, saying, "Surely I spoke of things I did not understand, things too wonderful for me to know. . . . My ears had heard of you but now my eyes have seen you. Therefore I despise myself and repent in dust and ashes" (42:3-6).

Here, Job demonstrates a new perspective on God and on his sufferings. He says, in effect, "Before I went through these sufferings, God, I had only heard of You. But now I've seen You with my own eyes! And because I now see reality from a new perspective, I despise myself and repent in dust and ashes." That's authentic repentance!

At the end of the book, Job glimpses the answer to the question of why good people suffer. The answer is that *there are no good people*. Yes, there are people who love God and put their trust in Him, and they receive His forgiveness as a gift of grace—but there are no good people. All have sinned, and no one is entitled to anything good from God. The suffering we endure is the result of living in a fallen world. The blessings we receive are the undeserved gifts of God's grace.

Keep Moving!

How should we respond when adversity comes into our lives? God gave us an example in the story of Israel's exodus from Egypt. After God inflicted plague after plague on Egypt, Pharaoh finally let the people of Israel leave. But Pharaoh soon changed his mind and came after the Israelites with soldiers and chariots. So the people of Israel found themselves trapped between Pharaoh's troops and the Red Sea.

The Israelites found themselves in a situation that we can probably identify with: a seemingly unsolvable problem with danger on every hand—and no escape route. The Israelites did exactly what you and I so often do: They cried out in panic and complained to God! Hearing their complaint, God said to Moses, "Why are you crying out to me? Tell the Israelites to move on" (Exod. 14:15).

That's exactly what God says to you and me when we find ourselves trapped in a crisis: "Don't stop! Keep moving forward!" We can't see how God plans to rescue us any more than the Israelites could imagine that they could walk right through the Red Sea. But God always has a plan. Our job is to simply *keep moving!*

God wants to bring us to a place in which we willingly allow Him to do anything He chooses with our lives. We serve the One who says, "I am the LORD, and there is no other. I form the light and create darkness, I bring prosperity and create disaster; I, the LORD, do all these things" (Isa. 45:6-7).

When we suffer adversity, it's natural to complain and question God. But God doesn't want us to respond in a *natural* way. He is teaching us a *supernatural* response. When we are tempted to panic or surrender, we need to be aware of when God is telling us to stand still and when He is telling us to keep moving forward!

When bad things happen to God's people, God's people keep moving, because we know that all things ultimately work out for good for those who are called according to His purposes.

QUESTIONS FOR REFLECTION

1. Oswald Chambers wrote, "Whenever God gives a vision to a saint, He puts him, as it were, in the shadow of His hand, and the saint's duty is to be still and listen." Are you going through a time of darkness right now? Do you see your present experience as God's punishment or the shadow of God's hand of provision and preparation?

2. In your times of adversity, have you ever been visited by "Job's comforters"—people who claim that your problems are a punishment from God for sin in your life? Did you find such people to be helpful in pointing out your sin? Did you find them to be hurtful in accusing you of sins you never committed? When you see others going through adversity, what is the best way to help them?

3. Do you agree that it ultimately doesn't matter if the source of your affliction and adversity comes from God or from Satan? Explain your answer.

4. Ultimately, we can never know (in this life) all the answers to our questions about suffering. How do you feel about that? Does unexplained suffering in your life make you doubt God? How can you answer the questions other people have when you don't have all the answers yourself?

5. What do you feel entitled to in life? What are some of the things that have happened to you that make you feel God is unfair—or that you are a victim?

6. What does the sacrifice of Jesus on the cross tell you about God's view of human suffering? What does it say to you about His love toward you? Does it help you, in times of affliction, to remember how Jesus suffered? Explain your answer.

Notes

1. Oswald Chambers, *My Utmost for His Highest: An Updated Edition in Today's Language*, ed. by James Reimann (Grand Rapids, MI: Discovery House Publishers, 1992), entry for January 19.

2. Billy Graham, *Answers to Life's Problems* (Nashville, TN: Word Publishing, 1988), pp. 251-252.

3. Bill Johnson, *When Heaven Invades Earth* (Shippensburg, PA: Destiny Image Publishers, 2003), p. 31.

4. "Swaziland: Politics," *Wikipedia.org*. http://en.wikipedia.org/wiki/Swaziland#Politics (accessed April 2006).

5. Allan Luks, "Helper's High: Volunteering Makes People Feel Good, Physically and Emotionally," *Psychology Today*, October 1988. http://www.findarticles.com/p/articles/ mi_m1175/is_n10_v22/ai_6652854 (accessed April 2006).

SUFFERING, SICKNESS AND SIN

*During the reign of David, there was a famine for three successive years;
so David sought the face of the LORD. The LORD said, "It is on account of Saul
and his blood-stained house; it is because he put the Gibeonites to death."*

2 SAMUEL 21:1

In his book *Thank God It's Monday*, my friend Rick Heeren tells about a couple who owned a struggling business. Their financial stress became so intense that they went to Rick for counseling. After listening to their story, Rick suggested that they pray together, adding that God was present in their midst because "where two or three come together in my name, there am I with them" (Matt. 18:20).

Rick then waited for a few moments to listen for the voice of God. It didn't take long. Within moments, a single word popped into Rick's mind: "Uriah."

Uriah was the husband of Bathsheba, the woman with whom King David committed adultery. He was the man that David arranged to have killed in order to cover up his sin of adultery. All of this sordid history was evoked in Rick's mind when he heard the word "Uriah." *Wow!* he thought. *What does all this have to do with the couple seated in front of me?*

After Rick prayed with the couple, he asked, "How did the two of you meet?" The answer they gave to him seemed vague and incomplete. "As we were praying," Rick said, "I received a word from the Lord. The word was 'Uriah.'"

Upon hearing that word, the wife broke down and began weeping. "Oh, Lord!" she cried, looking heavenward, "I knew You were going to make me confess all of these sins!"

Then the whole story spilled out. The woman had been married previously. During her first marriage, she had fallen in love with a man at the office where she worked—her current husband. Together, these two had worked out a scheme to get her first husband to give her a divorce and leave the company. Then the two adulterous schemers took over the company.

Of course, this woman hadn't arranged a murder as King David had when he arranged the death of Uriah. But she had betrayed and deceived her first husband—and she and her lover had stolen the company from him. Her first husband was truly her Uriah. Both she and her current husband had sinned against God, and their guilt had been gnawing at them ever since.

As the couple continued talking, they confessed to other sins. Rick realized that this couple didn't just have a business problem. They had a *sin* problem. God used their financial problems as a way of getting them to deal with their sin.

It's a biblical principle and a fact of life: Much of the adversity in our lives is a *direct* result of sin. Often, it's a simple matter of cause and effect. For example, if we are dishonest in the workplace, we can lose clients, be fired, or even be arrested. Sexual sins destroy families and produce unwanted pregnancies and sexually transmitted disease. Sins of gluttony, alcoholism and drug abuse take their toll on our health. Sins of anger and resentment can destroy relationships and shorten our lives. There is often an obvious relationship between sin and suffering.

But God sometimes brings about adversity in our lives that has no natural cause-and-effect connection. When this couple came to Rick with their financial problem, they didn't connect that problem in their minds with their concealed sins. Perhaps if they had made that connection, their fear of exposure would have kept them from going to counseling. But God in His mercy afflicted this couple with a failing business so that they would go to Rick. God then gave Rick the word "Uriah" to bring their sin problem into the open.

Our loving God must sometimes hurt us in order to heal us. In fact, this is almost always the case when our suffering is the result of sin.

Six Reasons for Adversity

From my Christian journey and my study of the Scriptures, I have identified six reasons for the adversity in our lives.

1. Our Sonship

Our Heavenly Father sometimes uses adversity to produce growth and maturity in His children. The book of Proverbs tells us, "My son, do not despise the LORD's discipline and do not resent his rebuke, because the LORD disciplines those he loves, as a father the son he delights in" (3:11-12). In Hebrews we read, "Endure hardship as discipline; God is treating you as sons. For what son is not disciplined by his father?" (12:7).

2. Our Identification with Others

God sometimes uses adversity in our lives to enable us to better understand and minister to other suffering people. Paul tells us that God "comforts us in all our troubles, so that we can comfort those in any trouble" (2 Cor. 1:4). God has placed all of us into a community—the Church—in which we are a part of one another. As Paul writes, "If one part suffers, every part suffers with it; if one part is honored, every part rejoices with it" (1 Cor. 12:26).

3. Our Testing

As we have already seen, God takes us through the Judas Test, the Integrity Test, the Perseverance Test and the Success Test in order to determine if we are ready for a leadership role in His kingdom. "These [trials] have come so that your faith—of greater worth than gold, which perishes even though refined by fire—may be proved genuine" (1 Pet. 1:7).

4. Our Calling and Preparation

Adversity teaches us how to endure pressure, problems and stress. "Consider it pure joy, my brothers, whenever you face trials of many kinds, because you know that the testing of your faith develops perseverance. Perseverance must finish its work so that you may be mature and complete, not lacking anything" (Jas. 1:2-4).

5. Our Ability to Trust God's Faithfulness

Adversity is a school of faith where we learn to trust God and depend on Him completely to provide for our needs. As Paul tells us, "God is faithful; he will not let you be tempted beyond what you can bear" (1 Cor. 10:13).

6. Our Sin

Sometimes, we experience adversity because God is dealing with sin in either our individual lives or in our corporate lives. This is the kind of adversity experienced by the couple who went to see Rick Heeren for counseling. God was lovingly dealing with this couple because of the sin they had tried to cover up.

Although the Scriptures clearly teach us that trials are a part of every believer's walk, we must be equally clear on this biblical principle: *Sometimes the adversity that comes into our lives is the direct result of sin.* When we suffer because of sin, we need to listen to what God is telling us through our adversity—and we need to change the direction of our lives.

When God Says, "Change Direction!"

In 2 Samuel 21, we see a tragic example of adversity resulting from sin when a famine came upon Israel during King David's rule. After the famine had continued for three years, David went before God and prayed for an answer. The word of the Lord came to David: "It is on account of Saul and his blood-stained house; it is because he put the Gibeonites to death."

You may remember the Gibeonites. They were the group of Canaanite people who fooled Joshua and the Israelites with the Gibeonite Ruse. From the time of Joshua to the time of King Saul, the Gibeonites had served Israel as woodcutters and water-carriers. Under Joshua, the Israelites had sworn never to harm the Gibeonites, but King

Saul had broken that pledge and had tried to annihilate all the Gibeonite people. Although Saul was dead, the stain of guilt remained upon the whole nation.

So King David called the surviving Gibeonites together and asked, "What shall I do for you? How shall I make amends?" The Gibeonites demanded the execution of seven of King Saul's male descendants. King David agreed, and the Gibeonites were avenged under the Old Testament system of justice—an eye for an eye. After that, the famine ended.

If we force God's hand through our own sin and rebellion, He will use adversity to bring us to repentance. As C. S. Lewis wrote in *The Problem of Pain*, "God whispers to us in our pleasures, speaks in our conscience, but shouts in our pains: it is his megaphone to rouse a deaf world."[1]

Someone once described suffering as God's manure for spiritual growth. Manure is not the most pleasant substance in the world, but we can't deny that it promotes growth. No matter what happens in our lives, we know that nothing happens without God's foreknowledge and permission. He always knows what we are going through—and why. God has a plan for the "manure" of our affliction. It is not a plan to hurt us, but to heal us and help us grow.

A friend of mine once shared an illustration of the process God uses to change our direction in life. "If you were one of God's children," he said, "and God had something He wanted you to do, He would first speak to you in a still, small voice. He'd call your name and softly say, 'Change direction.' If you didn't listen, He might tap you on the shoulder and say, 'Change direction.' If you still failed to listen, He would grab you by both shoulders and shout, 'Change direction!' Finally, if you still failed to get the message, He would knock you out of the chair and onto the floor. At this point, you would have to pay attention to what He says."

God will use pain in order to create a relationship with His creation. This statement may blow your theology. However, consider the fact that God allowed Jesus to experience incredible pain in order for Him to have a relationship with His creation. Consider how Jesus created a relationship with Paul—he blinded him and used a crisis in his life in order to build a relationship with him.

This is not God's first choice for His creation. Romans 2:4 reveals that God's preference is to show mercy and kindness: "Or do you show contempt for the riches of his kindness, tolerance and patience, not realizing that God's kindness leads you toward repentance?"

We often seek God to get out of our pain, but the truth is that we become lovers of God because of His response to our pain. Obedience will not last when the motivation is the removal of our pain. Obedience only lasts when the motivation is loving devotion.

When God told the prophet Jonah to go to Ninevah, Jonah boarded a boat going in the opposite direction. So God sent a storm into Jonah's path, and Jonah was cast overboard and swallowed by a great fish. He spent three days in the belly of that fish before the fish regurgitated him. When Jonah washed up on the shore, He was ready to go in God's direction.

Before the apostle Paul served Jesus, his name was Saul, and he persecuted Christians. While Saul was on the road to Damascus, intending to round up and imprison more Christians, God struck him blind—and got his attention. Saul was then willing to listen to the Lord.

God knows us intimately. He knows what it takes to motivate us to godliness. He knows every circumstance we face. As the psalmist wrote:

> O LORD, you have searched me
>   and you know me.
> You know when I sit and when I rise;
>   you perceive my thoughts from afar.
> You discern my going out and my lying down;
>   you are familiar with all my ways (Ps. 139:1-3).

Are you listening to what God is trying to say to you about your sins, your habits and the direction of your life? He's whispering to you now. Don't make Him shout to you. Don't make Him shake you or knock you down. Hear what He says to you. Turn your life in His direction.

Never Conceal a Sin

Did you know that even the Lord Jesus Christ had to learn obedience through adversity? You might think that Jesus never had to learn anything, much less obedience. But the book of Hebrews tells us, "Although He was a Son, He learned obedience from the things which He suffered. And having been made perfect, He became to all those who obey Him the source of eternal salvation" (Heb. 5:8-9, *NASB*).

You might ask, "Does the Bible really say that Jesus had to learn to obey God? Does that mean that He was a disobedient sinner before He learned obedience?" No, that's not what the Scriptures say. Jesus was never disobedient to God. Just a few verses earlier in the book of Hebrews, we read that Jesus was "tempted in every way, just as we are—yet was without sin" (4:15).

If Jesus never sinned, what does the passage mean when it says that He learned obedience? It means that when Jesus suffered affliction, He learned what a human being must go through in order to be obedient to the Father. He learned that obedience is difficult and that it requires us to deny many of our impulses, urges and desires. He learned all of these things as He went through His sufferings on Earth. Yet He learned them without ever committing sin.

Jesus learned obedience through His sufferings—and so do we. God allows adversity in our lives to teach us what it means to obey God's will. God has designed our trials to separate us from our attachment to sin and our former life. He uses our suffering to take us deeper into a relationship of trust and dependence on Him.

As I was going through the first few years of my Joseph Pit experience, God brought something to my attention: Much of my suffering was actually self-inflicted. It involved some deep-seated generational sins that had influenced the way I related to God and others. That realization drove me to seek God's strength in rooting out and destroying the sinful attitudes and habits in my life that were causing me pain and suffering. Once I got past my initial anger toward God, I realized that much of what I had interpreted as unjust punishment from God was actually His gracious attempt to remove those sins from my life. He was not trying to hurt me. He was trying to heal me.

That's the perspective God wants us all to learn, especially when we undergo trials that result from sin. God loves us in spite of our sins, but He also loves us too much to leave us in our sins. As the apostle Peter tells us, "Therefore, since Christ suffered in his body, arm yourselves also with the same attitude, because he who has suffered in his body is done with sin. As a result, he does not live the rest of his earthly life for evil human desires, but rather for the will of God" (1 Pet. 4:1-2).

The book of Proverbs tells us, "Misfortune pursues the sinner, but prosperity is the reward of the righteous" (13:21). We find one of the clearest examples of this principle in the tragic story of King David found in 2 Samuel 11 and 12.

David made a number of seemingly minor choices that snowballed into an avalanche of suffering, shame and tragedy. It started when he chose to stay at home in Jerusalem instead of going out to lead his troops into battle, as was his duty. David had too much time on his hands, which ultimately led to him committing adultery with Bathsheba and trying to cover up that sin with murder. One sin led to a worse sin, which led to an even worse sin, and on and on.

God had placed David on the throne, but David began to neglect his duties and misuse his power. Although David thought that he had concealed his sin by arranging the death of Bathsheba's husband, God knew what David had done. God in His love would not allow David's sin to remain hidden.

So God sent the prophet Nathan to tell King David a story: "There were two men in a town, one rich, one poor. The rich man had many sheep and cattle. The poor man had nothing but one little ewe lamb, which he raised like one of the family. The ewe lamb shared the man's food, drank from his cup, and slept in his arms. One day, when the rich man had a guest to entertain, he didn't want to slaughter any of his own sheep or cattle, so he took the poor man's lamb, killed it, and prepared it as a feast for his guest."

Hearing the story, King David was furious. "The rich man deserves death!" he said. "He must pay the man four times the value of the lamb, because he did an unjust thing and had no compassion!"

Then Nathan pointed his finger at King David and said, "*You* are the man! This is what the Lord, the God of Israel says: 'I anointed you king over Israel, and I delivered you from the hand of Saul. I gave your master's house to you, and your master's wives into your arms. I gave you the house of Israel and Judah. And if all this had been too little, I would have given you even more. Why did you despise the word of the Lord by doing what is evil in His eyes? You struck down Uriah the Hittite with the sword and took his wife to be your own!'"

David's sins were laid bare. To his credit, David confessed and repented of his sins, and God forgave him. But God also told David that there would be lasting consequences for his sin. God's forgiveness restores the broken relationship between Himself and the sinner, but forgiveness can't make everything exactly as it was. Sin has consequences that forgiveness cannot change.

The story of King David's attempt to conceal his sin illustrates truths that are recorded throughout Scripture: "He who conceals his sins does not prosper, but whoever confesses and renounces them finds mercy" (Prov. 28:13), and, "Do not be deceived: God cannot be mocked. A man reaps what he sows. The one who sows to please his sinful nature, from that nature will reap destruction; the one who sows to please the Spirit, from the Spirit will reap eternal life" (Gal. 6:7-8).

How to Lose a Kingdom

Sin hinders prayer. God tells us that the "prayer of a righteous man is powerful and effective" (Jas. 5:16), but when we sin, God hides His face from us and does not hear our prayers—except, of course, our prayers of confession and repentance. "But your iniquities have separated you from your God," said the prophet Isaiah. "Your sins have hidden his face from you, so that he will not hear" (Isa. 59:2).

We see this principle in the life of King Saul. In 1 Samuel 15, God tells Saul through the prophet Samuel to attack Israel's enemies, the Amalekites. God's instructions are clear and specific: Destroy everything, even the Amalekites' herds and flocks. So Saul gathers his army and attacks the Amalekites, but he doesn't follow God's instructions.

Instead, he keeps the best of the sheep and cattle for himself.

So God tells the prophet Samuel, "I am grieved that I have made Saul king, because he has turned away from me and has not carried out my instructions." Samuel prays and weeps before God all night, and then in the morning goes to Saul to confront him.

As Samuel approaches, Saul lies, "I have carried out the Lord's instructions."

Samuel replies, "Then why do I hear sheep bleating and cattle lowing?"

Saul, thinking quickly, shifts the blame. "The soldiers brought the animals from the Amalekites. They spared the best of the sheep and cattle to sacrifice to the Lord your God, but we totally destroyed the rest." Of course, Saul fails to mention that the soldiers acted on *his* orders. By saying that the animals will be sacrificed to God, Saul believes that his act of disobedience will be okay.

"Stop!" Samuel says, not wanting to hear any more lies. "Let me tell you what the Lord said to me last night. The Lord anointed you king over Israel. He sent you on a mission to completely destroy those wicked people and wipe them out. Why did you disobey the Lord? Why did you take the plunder that God told you to destroy?"

When King Saul again says that he intends to sacrifice the animals to God, Samuel replies, "To obey is better than sacrifice, and to heed is better than the fat of rams. For rebellion is like the sin of divination, and arrogance like the evil of idolatry. Because you have rejected the word of the Lord, he has rejected you as king."

It's important to note that Saul wasn't rejected as king because he overtly rebelled against God. He simply thought that he could serve God in his own way—through his own rules—and ignore any of God's commands that seemed inconvenient. King Saul thought that it would be wasteful to carry out God's commands to the letter, so he obeyed what he wished to obey, disobeyed the rest, and tried to make it all okay by sacrificing some of the plunder to God. But God cannot be mocked. We reap what we sow.

That is how Saul lost a kingdom. And you and I can lose our kingdoms, our positions of leadership, and our usefulness to God in the very same way.

We also need to be aware that God will sometimes use Satan to weed sin out of our lives. We see this in Paul's letters to the Christians at Corinth. Paul heard of a man in the Corinthian church who openly engaged in sexual sin. Even worse, the church had become proud of its tolerance of a sin that even the pagans found shameful. So Paul told the Corinthian church:

> When you are assembled in the name of our Lord Jesus and I am with you in spirit, and the power of our Lord Jesus is present, hand this man over to Satan, so that the sinful nature may be destroyed and his spirit saved on the day of the Lord (1 Cor. 5:4-5).

Notice that Paul instructs the Corinthians to hand this man over to Satan—*not* destroy the man's soul and condemn him to eternal punishment—so that the man's "sinful nature may be destroyed and his spirit *saved* on the day of the Lord." Although it sounds paradoxical, *because of His love for us, God will actually allow Satan to afflict us.*

Shortly before going to the cross, Jesus said to Simon Peter, "Simon, Simon, Satan has asked to sift you as wheat. But I have prayed for you, Simon, that your faith may not fail. And when you have turned back, strengthen your brothers" (Luke 22:31-32). Notice that Satan must first ask God's permission to afflict a believer. This is true whether that believer is Job or Simon Peter or you or me.

Notice, too, that even though God gave Satan permission to "sift" Simon Peter, Jesus prayed that Peter's faith would withstand Satan's attack. Jesus prays the same prayer for us.

God's goal when He hands a believer over to Satan is to *restore* that believer, not destroy him. We see the effect of this form of affliction in Paul's second letter to the Christians at Corinth. When Paul writes this second letter, the Corinthians have done as Paul instructed in his first letter: They have handed the immoral man in their fellowship over to Satan by expelling him from the church. Now the man has confessed and repented. So Paul writes:

> The punishment inflicted on him by the majority is sufficient for him. Now instead, you ought to forgive and comfort him, so

that he will not be overwhelmed by excessive sorrow. I urge you, therefore, to reaffirm your love for him (2 Cor. 2:6-8).

Friend, if you find yourself enmeshed in sin right now, I urge you to repent and turn to God. Don't lose your kingdom because of sin. Don't give Satan a handle on your life so that he can sift you as he sifted Simon Peter. God will not bless an unrighteous life, but He is willing and eager to bless the humble and contrite heart. As the apostle John tells us, "If we confess our sins, he is faithful and just and will forgive us our sins and purify us from all unrighteousness" (1 John 1:9).

Sickness and Sin

One summer day back in 1967, 17-year-old Joni Eareckson was swimming with her sister in the Chesapeake Bay when she decided to dive off of a raft. She thought the water was deep enough, but she was wrong. When her head hit the bottom, the impact crushed her fourth cervical vertebrae. Joni's sister saw her hair floating at the surface, jumped in, and pulled her out. Joni has been a quadriplegic ever since.

At the time of the accident, Joni had just graduated from a Baltimore-area high school and had her bags packed for Western Maryland College. Ironically, she planned to be a physical therapist. (She later said, "I got into physical therapy—but on the wrong end.")

Joni sought God's healing for years, but to no avail. As she learned to accept her paralysis, God used her to demonstrate His power and grace to millions of people around the world. Today, Joni is an extraordinarily gifted painter, even though she can only paint with the brush held in her teeth. She speaks and sings before audiences, has written dozens of books, and has an award-winning daily radio program.

Joni's life has been so full that people often assume she feels better off being paralyzed than able to walk. But that's not true. She's been able to impact more lives from her wheelchair than she ever could have on her own two feet, yet she still would like to walk, run, swim and dance. As she once told CNN talk show host Larry King, "I can't wait for heaven to get hands that work and feet that walk. . . . I'll not only jump up, dance, kick, do aerobics, but I'll paint big, splashy murals."[2]

Even though God can turn our afflictions into blessings for our own lives and the lives of others, affliction is still affliction. Suffering is still suffering. Sickness and injury are never easy to endure, even when we can see God's purpose in it. From Scripture and my own observation of the world, I have concluded that the physical illnesses that afflict us can be traced to one of four principal sources.

1. Sickness Can Glorify God

God sometimes allows sickness to bring glory to Himself and to teach us more about His power and love. In John 11, Jesus' friend Lazarus became sick and died. When Jesus received the news that Lazarus was sick, He said, "This sickness will not end in death. No, it is for God's glory so that God's Son may be glorified through it" (v. 4).

Jesus and His disciples went to Bethany, the town where Lazarus lived. When they arrived, they were told that Lazarus had been dead for four days. Why did Jesus wait to come until four days after His friend's death? It was probably because there was a Jewish tradition that held that when a person died, his spirit hovered around the grave for three days, hoping to be reunited with the body. Jesus deliberately waited four days to dispel any hope that Lazarus might live again.

When Jesus arrived at the tomb and found the sisters and friends of Lazarus mourning and weeping, He wept with them (He always mingles His tears with ours). Then He said, "Take away the stone. . . . Did I not tell you that if you believed, you would see the glory of God?" (vv. 39-40).

The people rolled away the stone. Jesus prayed and then called into the tomb, "Lazarus, come out!" And Lazarus came out, still bound in his grave clothes. Jesus told the friends of Lazarus, "Take off the grave clothes and let him go" (v. 44). The word of the miracle spread all around the region.

What was true in Jesus' day is still true in ours: God sometimes allows sickness to enter our lives in order to bring glory to Himself and to teach us more about Him. The psalmist spoke of this same principle when he wrote, "It was good for me to be afflicted so that I might learn your decrees" (Ps. 119:71).

My friends Kita and John learned these truths in a deeper way when John became sick with an illness that required repeated hospitalization. Kita couldn't understand why John continually suffered with these illnesses. She wondered if it might be God's disciplining hand in John's life. What if John had sin in his life that he hadn't dealt with?

I wasn't even aware that Kita was struggling with such questions. However, one Saturday morning as I began my Bible study time, I was reading in John 9, where Jesus and His disciples encountered a man born blind. The disciples asked, "Rabbi, who sinned, this man or his parents, that he was born blind?" (v. 2). Jesus replied, "Neither this man nor his parents sinned, . . . but this happened so that the work of God might be displayed in his life" (v. 3). Then Jesus healed the man of his blindness.

As I read that passage, I felt a prompting within me to call Kita. I picked up the phone and called her house. She wasn't in (I later learned that she was at the hospital with John), so I left a message on her answering machine. "I've been reading in John 9," I said, "and I felt God urging me to call you . . ." and then I recounted the story for her. "I don't know if this story means anything special to you, but I felt the Lord wanted me to share it."

That night, Kita returned my call. "Os," she said, "that story was meant just for me! I have been sick with worry that John's illness might be the result of some sin in his life, but God used you to reassure me that He has another purpose for John's illness. In fact, you're not the only person who gave me that message today."

Kita then told me how John's doctor had told her that he thought John's illness was meant for God's glory—and that God wanted Kita to let go of her concerns about John's spiritual condition. So God used two of His servants to send Kita the same message. Within a few weeks, God healed John. He hasn't been back in the hospital since.

2. Sickness Can Be a Disciplinary Judgment

God sometimes allows sickness in our lives as a disciplinary judgment against sin. Paul tells us that some sickness can be traced to sin in our lives—especially the sin of taking communion without dealing with unrepented sin. Paul writes:

Therefore, whoever eats the bread or drinks the cup of the Lord in an unworthy manner will be guilty of sinning against the body and blood of the Lord. A man ought to examine himself before he eats of the bread and drinks of the cup. For anyone who eats and drinks without recognizing the body of the Lord eats and drinks judgment on himself. That is why many among you are weak and sick, and a number of you have fallen asleep [died]. But if we judged ourselves, we would not come under judgment. When we are judged by the Lord, we are being disciplined so that we will not be condemned with the world (1 Cor. 11:27-32).

Paul makes it clear that there is often a direct relationship between sin and the illnesses that sometimes take place among us in the Church. Does this principle still hold true today? Most definitely—and we should take this matter seriously. It's easy to maintain an image of righteousness that fools other Christians. But God is never fooled.

If you become ill, ask God to reveal whether or not this sickness is rooted in some sin in your life. If you realize that there are sins in your life that you haven't dealt with, then that's the place to begin.

A friend and mentor of mine who ran a Christian retreat center told me about an incident in which the Lord woke him early in the morning and told him to write a letter to a pastor—a man whom he didn't personally know. So my friend wrote the letter as God directed. In the letter, my friend told this pastor that if he didn't repent of his sin, he would die. My mentor didn't know what that sin might be. He only knew that the Holy Spirit had given him this message.

My mentor then shared the letter with a minister who knew the pastor in question. After reading the letter, this pastor said, "I would like to sign that letter, too." My mentor showed it to several other pastors, and they all asked to add their names to the letter. Finally, the letter was sent.

The pastor who received the letter did not repent of his sin. Within two years, he was diagnosed with cancer and died.

Is there a relationship between sin and sickness? I'm convinced of it. By the same token, there is a relationship between repentance and health. As we see in the letter of James, "the prayer offered in faith will make the sick person well; the Lord will raise him up. If he has sinned, he will be forgiven" (5:15). If you have hidden sin in your life, I urge you to deal with it, confess it, repent of it and live a healthy and joyful life as God intended.

3. Sickness Can Be an Affliction from Satan

Sometimes, the sickness in our lives is an affliction from Satan. Illness can come into our lives that has absolutely nothing to do with any sins we have committed. Satan is active in the world, and he seeks to hinder us and torment us any way he can. Remember, when Job was afflicted with boils from head to foot, it was an act of Satan. But remember, too, that Satan can only act with God's permission and within the boundaries and limits that God sets.

If you are ever afflicted by Satan, you can be sure of one thing: God will use that affliction to bring about His plan in your life, not Satan's plan. All things work together for good in the lives of believers, because God can turn even the works of Satan into something beautiful in our lives: greater maturity, deeper faith, and a closer walk with the Lord.

4. Sickness Can Be a Natural Part of Living in a Fallen World

No one lives forever. As we age, our bodies begin to break down, slow down and shut down. This is a natural process of living in a fallen world. As the time of our departure from this earth grows closer, God may allow illness to bring our lives to a close.

As I write these words, my mother is in her mid-eighties and suffers from dementia, a gradual deterioration of her memory accompanied by changes in her personality. My four sisters provide the primary care for her, and I regularly make the four-hour trip to visit her. My mother's illness has brought our family together in some ways and divided our family in other ways.

This season in my mother's life began in 2003 when she was admitted to the hospital for a back problem and dehydration. She had always been healthy, and her mind was always very sharp. We expected her to have a brief hospital stay and then return home to a normal life. But the doctors gave her too large a dose of medication for her 100-pound frame.

When our mother came out of the hospital, she was a different person. Her thoughts were confused, and she had trouble recalling the names of family members.

It has been heartbreaking to watch my mother's gradual deterioration. I often wish the Lord had a different way for people to exit this life—a way that didn't involve such a loss of dignity and change in personality. I sometimes wonder, *What is God seeking to accomplish in my mother's life through this time? What is He accomplishing in my life, and in the lives of other family members?*

Watching the slow progression of my mother's illness, I realize that the illnesses we suffer serve to loosen the attachments we have for this earthly life. Our infirmities make us long for heaven, both for ourselves and for our loved ones. I cling to the words of the apostle Paul: "Now we see things imperfectly as in a poor mirror, but then we will see everything with perfect clarity. All that I know now is partial and incomplete, but then I will know everything completely, just as God knows me now" (1 Cor. 13:12 *NLT*).

God Still Heals

I rejoice that God still heals our diseases! Some years ago, I flew to Kansas City for a speaking engagement. I had no sooner stepped off the plane when I received an emergency message from home. I called my wife, Angie, and learned that she had just experienced another episode of severe abdominal pain. "I think I need to go to the emergency room," she said.

"I'm coming straight home," I replied. I canceled my speaking engagement and boarded the next flight back to Atlanta.

Once in the air, I thought back to the time, more than a year earlier, when I had to rush Angie to the emergency room for the same symptoms. As soon as we arrived at the ER, Angie cried out and fell to the floor in a fetal position. The nurses seemed completely unfazed by her pain and told me, "She'll have to wait. We don't have any place to put her right now." (Since then, I think of the ER as the "No Hurry, You'll Get Over It" room.) We returned to the ER two more times that week because of the same issue, but the doctors couldn't diagnose her problem.

Angie endured repeated bouts of intense pain, two surgeries and countless diagnoses that turned out wrong or were disputed by other doctors. After 18 months, Angie showed little improvement. She had reached a point of discouragement that I had never seen before. Then I thought of my friend Ron in Cincinnati, who has the strongest prophetic gift of anyone I've ever known. "Angie," I said, "we need to call Ron. If there's anyone we can trust to hear what God is saying in this situation, it's Ron."

So I called Ron and explained the situation. He prayed for us over the phone, and then asked, "Have you and Angie ever been to Africa?"

"Yes," I said. "At the beginning of the year, we went to Egypt for a marketplace conference. Why?"

"I'm seeing a curse that was placed on you there. What did you do in Egypt?"

"We visited the Egyptian museums and pyramids. Some friends cautioned us to pray before we went into those places, because the demonic history is strong in that land. They said that we should be careful about spiritual forces that might be attached to things from that country. So we didn't bring back any souvenirs."

"Did you or Angie experience anything unusual after you returned?"

"Shortly after we got back, Angie started having trouble sleeping at night. No matter how tired she was or how many sedatives she took, she remained wide awake. And throughout this ordeal, she's been having recurring bouts of abdominal pain."

As we talked, Ron said that he saw Angie in the hospital hooked up to a diagnostic machine that gave the doctors a readout of her vital signs. Ron said that the diagnosis the doctors had given Angie was wrong, and he then began to describe Angie's symptoms in detail. At the end of our conversation, Ron prayed again and, in the name of Jesus, broke any curses that might have attached themselves to Angie.

Immediately after that phone conversation, Angie experienced marked improvement. Ever since that time, Angie has been steadily experiencing God's healing. Three months later, Angie had no more symptoms of sleeplessness or pain. Today, she is back to her old self.

I wondered, *Why would God allow Angie to experience such sickness?* Then the answer came to me: God was training Angie's hands for spiritual warfare. As the words of Psalm 144:1 tell us, "Praise be to the LORD my Rock, who trains my hands for war, my fingers for battle." During Angie's illness, several intercessors told us that a birthing was taking place in Angie's life regarding a ministry that she would have. I believe that she has been learning to do battle and that God is going to use her to help others through her victory over this medical condition.

Sometimes the sickness we suffer comes as a result of sin. We should always examine ourselves during times of illness to make sure that our lives are in tune with God. But sometimes sickness comes and we must just learn to battle by faith. Thank God, He has promised to weave all of our sufferings into a beautiful tapestry of ministry and praise. Our God is an awesome God!

QUESTIONS FOR REFLECTION

1. Are you going through a time of adversity right now? Which of the six possible reasons for your affliction listed in this chapter do you think best explains the adversity you are facing right now? (It's okay to select more than one.) Explain your answer.

2. As C. S. Lewis wrote in *The Problem of Pain*, "God whispers to us in our pleasures, speaks in our conscience, but shouts in our pains: it is his megaphone to rouse a deaf world." Was there ever a time when God had to shout at you through His megaphone? How did God get your attention? What was the result?

3. Was there ever a time in your life when you concealed a sin? What was the effect of that hidden sin in your life? Was that sin ever exposed? How did you feel when it was revealed? Were you devastated—or relieved?

4. In 1 Samuel 15, we see that King Saul lost a kingdom because he failed to follow God's instructions. What is the kingdom that you stand to lose? Are you keeping God's commandments, or are you putting your kingdom at risk?

5. Are you experiencing an illness right now? If not, think back to the last illness you had. What do you think is God's purpose in your illness? Explain your answer.

Notes

1. C. S. Lewis, *The Problem of Pain* (San Francisco: HarperSanFrancisco, 2001), n.p.
2. Joni Eareckson Tada, interview with Larry King on *CNN Larry King Live*, August 3, 2004. http://transcripts.cnn.com/TRANSCRIPTS/0408/03/lkl.00.html (accessed April 2006).

1 1

ADVERSITY RESULTING FROM STRONGHOLDS

For though we live in the world, we do not wage war as the world does. The weapons we fight with are not the weapons of the world. On the contrary, they have divine power to demolish strongholds.

2 CORINTHIANS 10:3-4

My attorney called me and said, "I just got off the phone with John."

John was my friend and business associate in another city. He and I were working out an agreement for a business partnership, and I had asked my attorney to call him to iron out the last few details of the agreement. Everything in the agreement was simple and straightforward, so I didn't anticipate any problems. But the tone in my attorney's voice told me that something was wrong.

"How did your conversation go?" I asked.

"Not too well. Your friend was angry about something, but for the life of me, I don't know what I said that set him off."

"Please give it another try," I said.

The next day, my attorney called back and reported the same results.

"Okay," I said. "Let me talk to John."

The next day, I drove to John's town, 90 minutes away, and we sat down together to review our partnership agreement. It wasn't long before John began complaining about my attorney. Yet all of his complaints were vague and general. He saw my attorney as pushy, arrogant and deceptive—not at all the man I knew him to be. The more John talked, the angrier he got. I urged him to calm down. He ignored my pleas. There was no reasoning with him.

Finally, I shouted, "John, in the name of Jesus I rebuke that spirit of insecurity and fear that is driving you right now!"

John sat back and stared at me. I'm a very soft-spoken person, and John never imagined that he would hear such a thing coming from me. Frankly, I was a bit surprised myself, but it needed to be said.

"John," I said, "I think I know what's going on here. Years ago, you lost millions of dollars due to a corporate takeover directed by attorneys. You're reacting to old hurts. My attorney isn't trying to railroad you. You need to let go of past hurts and see this agreement for what it is. It's fair to both of us."

My friend took a deep breath. "You're right, Os. I didn't realize it, but that's exactly what was happening. I've been tricked by slick attorneys in the past and I unconsciously thought that it was happening all over again. I guess I owe you an apology—and your attorney as well."

John signed the agreement and everything went smoothly after that.

Years later, I learned about a spiritual principle underlying this conflict with my friend John: We sometimes experience adversity due to *spiritual strongholds*.

What Are Spiritual Strongholds?

The word "stronghold" means "fortress." In the spiritual realm, strongholds are hidden and fortified places in the soul where demonic and destructive ideas can take hold of a person without that person being aware of it. Strongholds control our actions and destroy our relationships by ruling and directing the way we think. Because strongholds are hidden, we are unaware of them until other people point them out to us or until a major crisis forces us to examine the root causes of our problems.

There's a common pattern to the development of spiritual strongholds within an individual. That sequence looks like this:

1. Destructive *thoughts* are introduced to the mind of an individual (usually from a satanic source), which become negative beliefs.

2. The individual contemplates these destructive thoughts and beliefs, which in turn produce destructive *emotions*.

3. Destructive emotions prompt the individual to take destructive *actions* (including speaking hurtful words to others).

4. This cycle repeats until destructive actions form destructive *habits*.

5. As the habit becomes harder and harder to break, a *stronghold* is built. Once this occurs, Satan has a base of operation—a hidden fortress—established within the soul of that person.

You may be thinking, *Why haven't I been aware of spiritual strongholds in my life?* The answer: Spiritual strongholds are hidden and difficult to detect with your conscious mind. Your strongholds actually form part of your mental filter of reality. A stronghold involves unexamined assumptions—beliefs that you assume to be true, though they may be utterly false.

Imagine being born with blue-tinted sunglasses over your eyes. You would grow up looking at the world through a blue filter. The people around you would appear to have blue skin, the walls of your home would be blue, your dog and cat and goldfish would be blue. The fact that the whole world was tinted blue wouldn't seem strange to you. It would seem normal.

That's what a stronghold is like. It's a set of ideas and assumptions that seem normal to you. Everything you perceive about the world is filtered through those ideas and assumptions. You don't know that there is any other way of looking at reality because this filtered reality is all you've ever known.

Now imagine taking those blue-tinted glasses off for the first time. Suddenly, you are able to see colors you've never known before: bright white, vibrant yellow, warm red, fiery orange, emerald green. It's as if a whole new world has opened up to you. That's what it's like when, through the power of God, you are finally able to demolish the strongholds that have blinded you to reality and truth.

God created each of us with seven basic needs. Although there is no place in Scripture where these seven needs are listed per se, we find all seven illustrated in Genesis 1 and 2. Those seven basic human needs are:

1. Dignity
2. Authority
3. Blessing and provision
4. Security
5. Purpose and meaning
6. Freedom and boundary
7. Intimate love and companionship

Whenever we seek to meet one or more of these basic physical or emotional needs outside of God's design for our lives, we set the stage for the development of a generational stronghold. Strongholds form when we try to meet our needs in ways that are contrary to God's will. Strongholds are part of Satan's strategy for deceiving us into conforming to the pattern of this fallen world. God wants to break us of our conformity to this world by totally transforming and renewing our minds and hearts. He seeks to demolish the strongholds that hold our minds captive to satanic deception.

Strongholds in the Bible

In the Gospel of Matthew, there are two parallels that most students of the Bible fail to notice. The first of these two parallels is in Matthew 4, the story of the temptation of Jesus by Satan. In that passage, Jesus has just been baptized, and He goes out into the wilderness to fast and pray. There, Satan comes to Him with three temptations. In the third and final temptation, Satan takes Jesus to a high mountain, shows Him all the kingdoms of the world, and then offers them to Jesus if He will bow down and worship Satan. Jesus replies, "Away from me, Satan!" (v. 10).

The second parallel passage is in Matthew 16. Simon Peter has just made his famous confession of faith, "You are the Christ, the Son of the living God!" (v. 16) and Jesus has blessed him and renamed him Peter, "the Rock." This is the high point in Simon Peter's career as a disciple. But immediately after He says this to Peter, Jesus tells him and the other disciples that He is going to suffer and die. Peter objects, "Never, Lord! . . . This shall never happen to you!" (v. 22).

Now, here's where we find the second parallel: Jesus replies to Peter, "Get behind me, Satan! You are a stumbling block to me; you do not have in mind the things of God, but the things of men." (v. 23). Look again at the words of Jesus: "Away from me, Satan!" "Get behind me, Satan!" Jesus issued almost identical commands, first to Satan, then to Peter. The reason Jesus said such a shocking thing to His dear friend Peter was that He wanted to get through to Peter. Jesus knew that Satan was influencing Peter to speak those words. Satan had a stronghold in Peter—a stronghold of willfulness and pride that Peter didn't even know he had. That's why proud, impulsive Peter tried to talk Jesus out of His mission! Satan was talking through Peter and trying to use him to turn Jesus aside from His mission.

Jesus recognized the true source of Peter's words. The source was Satan, speaking from the stronghold. So Jesus answered Satan with the same command He spoke in the wilderness: "Get behind me, Satan!"

This illustrates how Satan uses strongholds in our lives. He hides within the deceptive mind-sets, false ideas, sinful habits and destructive practices that take root in our lives. We think that these ideas, habits and practices meet our physical and emotional needs. But the voice that whispers to us from our strongholds is the voice of Satan. Author and speaker Francis Frangipane, in his book *The Three Battlegrounds*, describes how strongholds develop in our lives:

> The Apostle Paul defines a stronghold as "speculations, a lofty thing raised up against the knowledge of God" (2 Corinthians 3:5). A demonic stronghold is any type of thinking that exalts itself above the knowledge of God, thereby giving the devil a secure place of influence in an individual's thought-life.

In most cases, we are not talking about a "spirit-possession." This author does not believe that a Christian can be possessed, for when a person is "possessed" by a demon, that demon fills their spirit the way the Holy Spirit fills the spirit of a Christian.

However, Christians can be oppressed by demons, which can occupy unregenerate thought-systems, especially if those thoughts are defended by self-deception or false doctrines! The thought, "I cannot have a demon because I am a Christian," is simply untrue. A demon cannot have you in an eternal, possessive sense, but you can have a demon if you refuse to repent of your sympathetic thoughts toward evil. Your rebellion toward God provides a place for the devil in your life.[1]

We may bristle at the idea that Satan could ever gain a foothold in our lives through a spiritual stronghold. We may want to reject the idea that we could ever be so deceived as to have a satanic voice whispering lies to us from a hidden stronghold within our souls. But remember this: It was only moments after Peter confessed Jesus as the Messiah, the Son of the living God, and only moments after Jesus blessed Peter and gave him his new name that Jesus had to rebuke Peter and say, "Get behind me, Satan!"

The issue of spiritual strongholds in our lives is a serious matter. We need to give heed to the dangers posed by the hidden strongholds in our lives—or risk giving Satan a fortress in which he can maintain a deadly presence in our lives.

Strongholds and Generational Influence

I used to share an office with a friend named Jim. We were both meeting with a mentor, Frank and learning spiritual principles from the Scriptures. Frank had spent a lot of time talking with us about spiritual strongholds. Through those discussions, I was learning that I had a stronghold in the area of insecurity and fear, and that this stronghold was having a corrosive influence on my life. Jim, meanwhile, was discovering that he had a stronghold of rebellion and pride.

Our mentor suggested that Jim call his mother to see if some of the symptoms he had found in his own personality were common in other family members. Jim was reluctant to call her, but Frank thought it was important, so Jim made the call. When his mother answered, Jim briefly explained the concept of spiritual strongholds. "Mom," he said, "Frank thinks I have a stronghold of rebellion. Do you see this in me?"

"Of course I do," she replied. "Our whole family has it!"

Jim was surprised. He had never seen this in himself, yet to those who knew him well it was as plain as day! As Jim questioned his mom further about her view of him, a picture emerged of a man with a strong-willed, stubborn spirit. Next, Jim called his brother and asked the same questions—and his brother gave him identical answers. Jim had to agree that he had a stronghold of rebellion.

Then Jim called his ex-wife. Despite their divorce, Jim and his ex had maintained a cordial relationship. He trusted her honesty. He asked her the same questions, and most of her answers were consistent with the ones given by his family. Then Jim asked his ex-wife to score him, on a scale of 1 to 10, on his anger. She scored Jim near the top of the scale. Jim was surprised. "Why did you score me so high?" he asked. "My mother and brother gave me low scores on anger."

"Ha-ha!" she chuckled wryly. "They weren't married to you!"

Jim frowned.

"By the way, Jim," she added, "may I score you on pouting?"

"Pouting?"

"You know, all those times when we had an argument and you would be silent and distant and I couldn't get through to you." She ranked him off the chart.

Jim was devastated. He set the phone down and prayed. In the strong name of Jesus, he renounced the stronghold of rebellion that had plagued him since childhood. As he did, he experienced a desire to yield himself fully to God and to serve others in God's name. Soon afterwards, he moved in with his widowed mother. As he talked and prayed with her, she began experiencing release from the spiritual strongholds in her own life.

A few years ago, I was having dinner with two Christian ladies from Singapore. One of them asked, "How do strongholds work? And how can a person be delivered from their destructive influence?"

"Let me ask you something," I said. "What was your relationship with your father like?"

She looked at me in surprise. "That's a strange question!" she said.

"It has a lot to do with the issue of strongholds," I said. I had noticed that she was a driven, aggressive businesswoman who spoke with intensity about her career. Behind the intensity, I sensed insecurity.

"Well," she said, "my relationship with my father was not a happy one." She went on to tell me how her father continually shamed her as she was growing up. He criticized her for being overweight and told her that she would never amount to anything. As she talked, her face hardened and she grew angrier and angrier.

After listening to her for a while, I said, "It sounds to me as though you were always seeking your father's approval—and that you still are. All your drive and ambition are focused on proving that you *do* amount to something so that you can win your father's approval. Everything you do comes from a stronghold of insecurity, fear of failure and fear of rejection. And your father was the same way—driven, fearful and insecure. Perhaps he spent his life trying to win *his* father's approval. You may be dealing with life the same way."

She nodded and tears came to her eyes. Once she agreed that she had a stronghold of insecurity, fear and rejection, I was able to pray for her deliverance. From that day forward, she began to experience freedom and joy in an area of her life that had plagued her for years.

As these incidents illustrate, strongholds tend to be passed down from one generation to the next. We see this principle at work in the lives of a father, a son and a grandson in the Old Testament—Abraham, Isaac and Jacob. All three of these men exhibited tendencies to deceive others in order to protect themselves. None of them thought there was anything wrong with it. Because of the stronghold of deception, they thought lying was a perfectly acceptable means of self-defense. All of this led to unnecessary adversity in their families:

While journeying in Egypt, Abraham lied about his wife. Sarah, saying she was his sister, because he was afraid the Egyptians would kill him for his wife. Isaac followed the same pattern when he claimed that his wife, Rebekah, was his sister. Rebekah schemed with her favorite son, Jacob, to deceive Isaac and Jacob's brother, Esau. Throughout Jacob's life, he manipulated people and circumstances with deception. Despite this flaw in Jacob's integrity, God saw something good in Jacob. Over time, He delivered Jacob from the stronghold of deception and control.

We see a similar pattern in the family of King David—only in David's case, the stronghold was sexual immorality. David traced his lineage to Rahab the harlot, who protected the spies of Israel when they came into the Promised Land. David's failures were often sins of the flesh (his adultery with Bathsheba, for example). David's son Absalom committed sexual immorality with David's concubines as an act of rebellion against his father. Amnon, another of David's sons, committed incest with his sister. David's son Solomon married pagan women who turned his heart away from God.

One reason why so many Christians live defeated lives is because they have not dealt with the generational strongholds in their lives. These strongholds can take many forms: anger, rage, violence, abuse, alcoholism, drug abuse, sexual immorality, witchcraft, fear, insecurity, and so forth. A spiritual stronghold is any area of one's life that is out of control because it is under the control of unseen evil forces. A spiritual problem can't be solved by natural means. The only way to pull down a spiritual stronghold is with a greater spiritual force—the power of God Himself. Paul calls this "divine power to demolish strongholds" (2 Cor. 10:4)

The Stronghold of Control

Like most people, I had to learn about my own stronghold from friends, mentors, employees at my agency and family members. My stronghold was a common one in both Scripture and everyday life: control rooted in insecurity and fear.

The first step in confronting the stronghold of control is to recognize the problem. For many years, I was deceived by my stronghold and couldn't recognize it in my life. It took a catastrophe—my Joseph Pit experience—for me to see that the problem was within me and that it was a spiritual stronghold. *It often takes a crisis to force us to examine ourselves.*

The urge to control people and situations is at the heart of many of my broken relationships, including my first marriage. For years prior to our separation, my wife and I went from one Christian counselor to another. Although these counselors tried to apply biblical principles to our situation, they never got to the root issues that continually stoked the fires of conflict. I have come to believe that unless a counselor is able to deal with deep spiritual issues, such as spiritual strongholds, the counseling process is likely to fail.

It was only after my marriage ended in divorce that I learned about strongholds. By God's grace, I was able to see the spirit of control working within me. I began to discover other areas of my personality that kept me from becoming like Christ. Through prayer and counseling with wise fellow believers, I was able to understand and renounce this spirit of control.

I also began to understand that a controlling personality is a common stronghold. Men who are accused of being controlling almost always deny that they have such a problem. It usually takes a life-shattering crisis to force a man to see it and deal with it. As King Solomon once lamented, "There is a time when a man lords it over others to his own hurt" (Eccles. 8:9). That's what a controlling stronghold is like.

A controlling stronghold is also at the heart of a religious spirit. People with a religious spirit tend to be rigid and dogmatic, driven by guilt and fear, resistant to change and new ideas, arrogant and "holier than thou" toward people who believe differently, quick to argue, slow to admit faults, and focused more on rules than relationships.

When Jesus died to save us, He made salvation available to humanity as a free gift. All we have to do is receive the gift of God's grace. But it's hard for a person who is influenced by the religious spirit to receive grace. Instead, the religious spirit insists on creating controlled systems (religions) that are works-based attempts to gain God's favor. These systems of religious control invalidate the work of the cross.

We see the stronghold of control in Jacob's life. His name means "supplanter," "deceiver" or "manipulator," all of which suggest his controlling personality. Although Jacob believed in God, he continually tried to do God's will in his own way. He started by scheming with his mother, Rebekah, to deceive his father, Isaac, and steal the birthright from his brother, Esau. Jacob got a taste of his own medicine when he wanted to marry his beloved Rachel but was tricked by Rachel's father, Laban, into marrying Rachel's sister, Leah, first. Laban was a deceiver and a manipulator himself, and he deceived Jacob into giving him 14 years of free labor so that Jacob could marry his daughters. Jacob illustrates the biblical principle that the sin we sow is usually the sin we reap.

Later, God told Jacob to return to his family. Jacob, fearing the wrath of his brother, Esau, devised a scheme to protect himself. Although God had promised to protect him, Jacob insisted on staying in control and substituting his plan for God's. He split up his family and sent them ahead in two directions while he stayed back.

Meanwhile, an angel came to Jacob and wrestled with him. During this encounter, God dealt with Jacob's strong, controlling will. He disabled Jacob, putting his hip out of joint so that Jacob could do nothing but cling to God.

Jacob is a picture of the worldly minded (carnal) Christian who wants to serve God on his own terms. God needed to break Jacob's stubborn will, and the only way He could do so was by disabling Jacob and taking away his ability to control. It was God's way of forcing Jacob to cling to Him and trust Him as the source of his life. It also forced Jacob to deal with the generational stronghold that had broken the relationship with his brother, Esau.

After God disabled Jacob's hip, Jacob was broken and ready to be used by God. His stronghold of control was demolished. The Lord gave him a new name: Israel, which was a symbol of the transformation that God had brought about in his life. The name "Israel" can be interpreted as "he who wrestles with God" or "let God prevail."

As my friend Bob Mumford so aptly says, "Beware of any Christian leader who does not walk with a limp." The Lord wants to use us just as He used Jacob and just as He used Joseph. But He can only use us on His terms, not ours. He has to break our controlling will so that His will prevails. That's why we need our Joseph Pit experience. That's why we need to have our hip dislocated by God.

Traits and Sources of the Stronghold of Control

Where does the spiritual stronghold of control come from? Controlling personalities have the following common traits that contribute to this stronghold in their lives:

- Controllers are tremendously insecure. This may not be readily apparent, however, because they cover up their insecurity with a facade of egotism, arrogance and a selfish demand to be the one who reigns.

- Controllers were usually wounded at some time in their early years. They feel they must control their world to avoid getting hurt again. Controlling is a means of self-preservation.

- Controllers are distrustful and wary, and their distrust damages relationships.

- Controllers are prone to anger. They become frustrated when they feel they're losing control of a situation. When things go wrong, they blame others and justify themselves, even when the problem is their own fault.

- Controllers are afraid. They act big on the outside but feel small on the inside. They are always on the edge of panic for fear of losing control.

- Controllers respond inappropriately to situations. They overreact and become angry out of proportion to the provocation. They fly into a rage or become hysterical over minor problems. Their inappropriate responses wound others, resulting in strained or shattered relationships.

- Controllers were trained to control. They learned it in the home. It's not that they choose to be controlling; it's simply the only thing they know.

• Controllers run in families. The stronghold of control is generational in nature.

I learned about these traits of controllers as I was discovering my own
stronghold of control. As I mentioned, I couldn't see these traits in myself
until other people pointed them out to me—and even then, I had to fight
my way through layers of denial to see it. The demolishing of my stronghold couldn't take place until I had wrestled with God and He had put
my hip out of joint.

As God took me through that experience, I discovered a number of
controlling patterns in my personality that affected my life and relationships. I tried to control people around me so that they would not nega-
tively affect me. When people disappointed me, I became angry. When life
didn't go my way, I became afraid. I experienced the fear of failure, the
fear of not achieving my goals, and the fear of losing my image as a successful businessman and Christian leader.

People with the stronghold of control tend to have high or even unrealistic expectations. When their expectations aren't met, they become
frustrated, angry and sometimes abusive. The controlling person tends to
jealously defend his or her rights: "I have a right to be mad!" "It's my life
and I'll do as I please!" "I have a right to know what you're up to!"

When God dislocates a controlling person's hip and demolishes his
stronghold of control, that person no longer talks about rights and enti-
tlements. He no longer has unrealistic expectations about people and circumstances. People who have known me both before and after my Joseph
Pit crisis tell me that there has been a huge change in my personality. I
myself can see the difference in how I relate to God, to people and to
problems in my life. I'm grateful that God has done a deep work in me.

The apostle Paul experienced the demolishing of a control stronghold. He had once been a fire-breathing Pharisee, devoted to the rigid
enforcement of his dogmas. He would go miles out of his way—all the
way to Damascus—just to round up Christians and throw them in jail.

But after Paul was struck down by the power of God on the Damascus
road, he was never the same. He let go of his rigid demands and expectations. He was delivered from the religious spirit and the stronghold of

control. He became content no matter what his circumstances were. If a situation didn't go his way, he didn't fight it. He just looked for the lessons in it. He yielded himself to the control of God.

Renouncing and Demolishing

Bart Pierce was nine years old when his mother died suddenly from blood poisoning. For years, Bart hated God for taking his mother away. He stopped caring about schoolwork, and his behavior became disruptive and belligerent.

Bart lived in a beach town and took up surfing as a teen. Friends turned him on to drugs and alcohol when he was 13, and he often sneaked out and partied all night. He broke into houses, stole cars and sold drugs on the street.

Once, when Bart was 17, he stayed overnight at a friend's house. He awoke to the sound of a state trooper knocking on the door. The trooper brought news that Bart's father had died from choking on food. When Bart went home to console his stepmother, she threw him out of the house.

After that, Bart plunged more deeply into drugs and crime. One night, he was walking with his girlfriend when a car pulled up. Two armed men jumped out and forced Bart into the car. The men took him out on a country road and stood him up against a sign. One of the men pointed a gun toward him and fired—but the bullet hit the sign above Bart's head. "Next time," the gunman said, "I'll blow your brains out."

The experience made Bart think hard about his life. He knew that he was searching for something, but he didn't know what. Sometime later, he married his girlfriend, Coralee, and continued surfing, doing drugs and searching for meaning.

One day, a friend invited Bart and Coralee to church. It was Bart's first experience of a worship service, and he felt nervous and out of place. Yet the people in that church had something he wanted. He returned the next Sunday—and gave his life to Jesus.

Bart grew in his faith and experienced deliverance from the strongholds of drug abuse and alcoholism. He shared his story in churches and with people on the street. God used his testimony to change many lives, including the life of his wife, Coralee. She became a believer and a woman of prayer.

In 1981, Coralee told Bart, "The Lord told me we're moving to Baltimore."

"Baltimore!" Bart said. "There's no surfing in Baltimore!" He dismissed the idea.

The next Sunday, a man with a prophetic gift stopped him at church and said, "Bart, God has revealed to me that you are going to Baltimore."

Later, his pastor took him aside and said, "Bart, I sense God calling you to Baltimore."

Finally, Bart had to agree. So he and Coralee moved to Baltimore. In time, he became the pastor of Baltimore's Rock City Church, where he began an outreach to the inner city poor. He became known as the pastor who cared for people that no one else cared for. Under Bart's leadership, Rock City Church became a model of how God can transform a community through Christian compassion. Bart also established Global Compassion Network to serve the needs of the poor around the world. Global Compassion Network played a key role in providing relief to victims of Hurricane Katrina in 2005.

"Our generation is raising up a 'Joseph company,'" Bart says today. "God is preparing believers who will not be content to do things the old way. Under the leadership of the Holy Spirit, they are redefining the Church for a new day and age, and they're helping to bring in a great end-time harvest of souls."

Back in his car-stealing and drug-dealing days, Bart never imagined how God would use his life. However, before God could use Bart, He had to deliver him from the strongholds that led to his anger and drug abuse. God delivered Bart Pierce from the enemy's strongholds—and today, through Bart's life, He is delivering thousands more.

God has a plan for using your life in ways you can't even imagine right now. But first you need to be delivered from the generational issues that are hurting your relationships and robbing you of joy and effectiveness for God. If, while reading this chapter, you've become aware of the influence of a stronghold in your life, I urge you to deal with it now. Repent of it. Receive God's power to pull down that stronghold. In the strong name of Jesus, renounce that stronghold by praying this prayer:

Father, I renounce the spiritual stronghold that has been operating in my life. Continue to open my eyes and reveal to me the hidden areas of my life in which sin has a foothold. I accept the grace that You offer to me through the presence and power of Jesus Christ in my life and through His blood that was shed on the cross. In Jesus' name I pray. Amen.

As you go forth and live your life, be continually transformed by the renewing of your mind, as Paul told us in Romans 12:2. This is your best insurance against spiritual influences that do not come from God. As your relationship with Him deepens day by day, you'll grow stronger in your ability to resist the sabotage of Satan—and he will no longer be able to establish a stronghold in your life.[2]

QUESTIONS FOR REFLECTION

1. Has anyone ever pointed out a flaw, habit or hindrance in your personality that you couldn't see? Do you think that person was right or wrong about you? Have other people pointed out the same issue in your life?

2. How do you respond when people identify potential problem areas in your life? Do you defend yourself and deny that you have a problem? Or do you try to learn something new about yourself?

3. Why do you think other people can often see strongholds in our lives when we can't see them ourselves?

4. Why do you think there is so often a generational pattern to spiritual strongholds? In other words, how do you think a stronghold is transmitted from one generation to the next? Is there a genetic mechanism that accounts for this? Does environment account for it? Is there a spiritual principle that would account for it? Explain your answer.

5. Do you "walk with a limp"? How have you wrestled with God? What stronghold has God broken in your life?

6. Do you see the traits of a controller in your life? As you've been reading this chapter, has God brought to mind any other possible strongholds in your life? What is your next step in allowing God to demolish those strongholds?

Notes

1. Francis Frangipane, *The Three Battlegrounds* (Cedar Rapids, IA: Arrow Publications, 1989), pp. 71-72.
2. For further reading on spiritual strongholds, I recommend two books by Neil Anderson: *Victory Over the Darkness* (Regal Books, 2000) and *The Bondage Breaker* (Harvest House, 2000). I also recommend *Steps to Freedom in Christ* (Regal Books, 2004), an inventory booklet by Neil Anderson that will help you identify and demolish the strongholds in your life, and *Demolishing Strongholds* (Restoration Ministries, 1995), a practical workbook by Mike and Sue Dowgiewicz for pulling down spiritual strongholds. (You can visit www.marketplaceleaders.org to order these resources.)

PART IV

PREPARING FOR THE ADVENTURE AHEAD

1 2

OUR RESPONSE
TO ADVERSITY

*Consider it pure joy, my brothers, whenever you face
trials of many kinds.*

JAMES 1:2

I was 14 years old in September 1966. I was home watching *I Dream of
Jeannie* on television when the program was interrupted by a news bul-
letin: "Three prominent local businessmen have died in a plane crash in
the mountains of Tennessee."

That's how I learned of the death of my father.

It was difficult and painful growing up without a father. I loved and
needed my dad. I couldn't understand why God would take him away
from me so suddenly. I certainly didn't see the death of my father as a
"blessing" in any sense of the word.

Yet I have seen blessings come out of that terrible tragedy. In the
years since my father died, God has brought a number of men across my
path who have lost fathers at an early age. Because of my own loss, I had
an instant connection with others who suffered similar losses. We
shared an experience that other people couldn't fully understand.

During my separation and divorce, I experienced emotional suffering I had never known before—and which I never imagined that I could
withstand. Before I went through the loss of my marriage, I thought that

I could empathize with people who were going through a divorce. But I never really understood the pain of divorce until I went through it myself. I can't call my own experience of divorce a blessing, but I've seen God use my pain to bless the lives of other people.

When I sit down with men who are experiencing troubled marriages, I can understand them in a way no happily married man ever could. When I encourage them to work at their marriages, I speak with the authority of experience. When I tell a recently divorced man that there's life after divorce, he can believe it.

I can't say that it was a blessing to go through seven years of financial adversity, but God has used my trial to bring blessing to other people. When I meet someone who is going through a business failure or a financial loss, there's an instant bond between us of shared experience.

God can take our adversity—a heart attack, cancer, an automobile accident, violent crime, bankruptcy, the loss of a loved one—and transform that pain into blessing for the people around us. We come out of those experiences stronger and better able to comfort and encourage others. Although adversity is never a blessing, God in His grace can bring blessing out of our adversity.

Adversity to Test and Teach Obedience

Throughout the Old Testament, we see many situations in which God tests His people in order to determine if they will follow Him or follow the systems of this world. Joseph underwent the Judas Test, the Integrity Test, the Perseverance Test and the Success Test as part of his preparation for leadership.

The nation of Israel was tested many times during the 40-year sojourn in the wilderness: "Remember how the LORD your God led you all the way in the desert these forty years, to humble you and to test you in order to know what was in your heart, whether or not you would keep his commands" (Deut. 8:2).

You might ask, "Why does God need to test us? Doesn't He know everything, including what we would do in every situation?" Yes, God knows—but we don't! *God doesn't test us in order to find out something He doesn't already know. He tests us so that we can learn about ourselves and His love, power and faithfulness.*

In Genesis 22, God tested Abraham by commanding him to sacrifice his son Isaac on a mountain in the land of Moriah. Isaac was Abraham's only son by his wife, Sarah—the son God had promised to Abraham. By demanding that Isaac be sacrificed, God seemed to be nullifying His covenant of making a great nation of Abraham. How could God's promise be fulfilled if Isaac was dead?

God tested Abraham to reveal whether or not Abraham truly trusted His promise. Yes, God knew what Abraham would do, but He wanted Abraham to know as well. So God put Abraham to the test—and Abraham passed it. As Abraham raised the knife to sacrifice his own son, God stopped him and provided a sacrificial ram instead.

The psalmist writes, "Test me, O LORD, and try me, examine my heart and my mind" (Ps. 26:2). Every test involves obedience in one way or another. When God tests us, He reveals the true state of our hearts. Are we obedient to His will, or are we self-willed? We might *think* we know the answer, but we would never *truly* know unless we were tested.

Our testing is intended to teach us something about ourselves and about God's faithfulness. Sometimes, as in the case of Abraham and Isaac, God asks us to do things that go completely against human logic. Why? Because we need to learn that God's logic is higher than ours and His wisdom is deeper than ours. God wants us to obey Him even when His commands seemingly make no sense.

The Three Responses to Adversity

When we experience adversity, we generally respond in one of three ways: (1) we become angry; (2) we suck it up; or (3) we accept it with joy.

1. Anger

When adversity comes our way, we say, "Why me, Lord?" We become bitter and resentful and blame God and others for our problems. We view ourselves as victims and demand that God answer our accusing questions: "Why don't You love me, Lord? Why are You being unfair to me?"

We feel entitled to life, health, wealth and happiness.

2. Suck It Up

Another way we respond to adversity is by adopting a stoic attitude, repressing our emotions and simply "sucking it up." We lie to ourselves and say, "I'm persevering. I'm demonstrating endurance." In reality, we are merely isolating ourselves with a shell of false bravado. We don't meditate on God's love, we don't pray, we don't believe God really has anything good planned for us. We simply suck it up and tell ourselves, "This will soon be over. I'm a survivor."

Those who adopt a tough exterior and simply try to survive their adversity will never receive what God has planned for them. They will never learn the lessons God has for them. God's desire for us, in times of adversity, is that we come to know Him in a more intimate way. As Isaiah writes, "I will give you the treasures of darkness, riches stored in secret places, so that you may know that I am the LORD, the God of Israel, who summons you by name" (45:3). We can only find God's secret riches by going deeper in a relationship with Him.

3. Acceptance with Joy

This is the response God seeks from us. When adversity comes, we rest in His love and trust that He knows best. We realize that nothing can happen to us without His permission. If there is pain in our lives, we know it's because God deems it necessary for our growth or wishes to use our pain to minister to others.

When we walk through trials with acceptance and joy, we grow in Christian maturity. When we can thank God for what He is accomplishing in our lives, we have that inner joy that the prophet Nehemiah spoke of: "Do not grieve, for the joy of the LORD is your strength" (Neh. 8:10). This is also the joy the apostle James spoke of: "Consider it pure joy, my brothers, whenever you face trials of many kinds. . . . Blessed is the man who perseveres under trial, because when he has stood the test, he will receive the crown of life that God has promised to those who love him" (Jas. 1:2,12).

During my seven-year Joseph Pit experience, I spent the first two years in the anger and suck-it-up stages. It took me two long, miserable years to reach a place in which I could genuinely accept the adversity that I was experiencing with joy. It took me that long to become dead to the things to which I was attached. I still felt pain over my broken marriage and my shattered finances, but amid the pain, I had God's peace. I had confidence in Him. I knew that the Lord was still on the throne and sovereign over my circumstances.

Anger is a natural response to adversity. A stoic suck-it-up attitude is a natural response, too. But acceptance with joy is not natural. It's *supernatural*. It's not a response that we can summon up from somewhere in our personality. It's something we can only receive as a gift from the Comforter, the Holy Spirit.

Tucked away in a much-neglected corner of the Old Testament is a little prophetic book called Habakkuk. It tells how God revealed to the prophet Habakkuk that Israel was soon to be invaded by the Babylonians. Habakkuk knew that Israel was about to suffer intense adversity as part of God's loving discipline of His people. Habakkuk faced the looming national tragedy with an attitude of acceptance with joy. He wrote:

> Though the fig tree does not bud
>> and there are no grapes on the vines,
> though the olive crop fails
>> and the fields produce no food,
> though there are no sheep in the pen
>> and no cattle in the stalls,
> yet I will rejoice in the LORD,
>> I will be joyful in God my Savior (3:17-18).

If Habakkuk could be joyful in the face of a national calamity, then we can rejoice in the Lord no matter what comes our way.

Adversity That Reveals the Power of God

If you've ever waded into the ocean, you know that it's easy to stand knee-deep in the surf and enjoy the waves washing up around your knees.

There's no danger; you're in control of the situation. But if you paddle out to the deep water and the undertow starts dragging you away from the shore, you have a problem. You can no longer stand on your own two feet. You no longer control the situation. You're adrift, bobbing up and down on the waves, unable to go where you want to go. That's what the Joseph Pit experience feels like.

In Matthew 14, we read that Jesus, after feeding the 5,000, sent His disciples across the lake. While the disciples were out on the water, a storm arose and threatened to sink their boat. As the disciples were about to give up hope, they saw Jesus coming toward them, walking on the water through the storm. However, they didn't know it was Him. In their terror, they thought they were seeing a ghost!

Seeing their fear, Jesus said, "Take courage! It is I! Don't be afraid."

"Lord, if it's you," Peter said, "tell me to come to you on the water."

"Come," Jesus said.

So Peter got out of the boat and walked on the water toward Jesus.

I can imagine how pleased Jesus was to see Peter stepping out in faith, daring to do the impossible. As a friend once told me, "Faith is spelled R-I-S-K." I'm sure Jesus would have been far *more* pleased if *all* of the disciples had leaped out of the boat and walked to Him on the water!

But there was Peter, doing just fine—until he became unnerved by the wind and waves. The moment Peter took his eyes off Jesus, he began to sink and cried out, "Lord, save me!"

Jesus pulled him out of the water and saved him. "You of little faith," He said. "Why did you doubt?"

When Jesus sent His disciples out, He *knew* a storm was coming. God still sends us into the storms of life today. He knows what we need to go through in order for us to grow in our faith. All too often, we need a good, hard storm! Why do we need to experience storms? To learn the same lesson Peter learned: Nothing is impossible *as long as we keep our eyes on Jesus.*

For a while in my trial of adversity, I went through a lengthy period of time in which I didn't have an income. During that time, my fear grew until, after one evening prayer walk, the Lord said to me, "How long will you keep your eyes on your circumstances instead of on Me? Do you think I've brought you this far just to throw you into the water?" That was a moment of realization. I had been looking at the storm and the waves. I wasn't looking at the Lord.

One night during a support group for divorced men that I attended, the leader told us to keep our eyes on two men in the front of the room. One man represented Jesus, the other represented circumstances. "Keep your eyes on both people," the leader said. Then the two men started walking in opposite directions. It was impossible to see both at the same time. We had to focus on one or the other. God wants us to keep our eyes fixed on Him, not on our circumstances.

One big lesson that God taught me through adversity was that I could trust Him completely with my financial problems. When I was financially successful, I never truly had to depend on God. I thought I was living by faith, but I didn't know what faith was until I didn't know how I would pay my mortgage or put food on the table.

There was a time after my divorce and remarriage when my wife, Angie, and I were trying to decide how to handle a disputed obligation. A man said that we owed him $3,000, but I didn't agree. We withheld the money for a while in the hopes of bringing this man to the negotiating table—but to no avail.

Finally, we felt God was telling us to pay this man, even though we were struggling and it would deplete our savings to do so. My top client had just revised our contract, dramatically reducing our income. Then a number of household appliances and my wife's car broke down, requiring us to pay for expensive repairs. Even so, we decided to obey God and pay the $3,000 bill. It made no rational sense, but we knew what God was telling us.

I confess that I didn't have peace. In fact, I felt a great deal of anguish. But with Angie's support, I trusted God to provide a way out of the situation. God had provided a ram to Abraham so that he didn't have to sacrifice his son. He had provided manna in the wilderness when it seemed the people of Israel would die of hunger. That same God would provide for us. Two weeks before Christmas, we paid the money cheerfully and joyfully, eager to see how God would provide for our needs.

Angie and I had decided not to give each other Christmas gifts that year. But our Lord, the Giver of every perfect gift, was still in the business of blessing. As Paul wrote, "He who calls you is faithful, who also will do it" (1 Thess. 5:24, *NKJV*). God's gift came in the form of a phone call from the manager of our Marketplace Leaders Foundation, a new nonprofit entity I had formed so that people could support our ministry. "I have good news," she said. "A donor has just deposited $20,000 into your foundation."

I couldn't speak. I was too choked up. The Lord had done it again.

Why does God take us to a point where there is absolutely no way out? Is God sadistic? Does He want us to suffer? No. He loves us more than we can imagine. In fact, He loves us too much to allow us to be satisfied with a superficial, unrealistic faith. He wants us to have a robust, invincible, obedient faith that will take us to the very limits of our possibilities.

Three Spiritual Stages

There are three stages to the Christian life: the convenience stage, the crisis stage, and the conviction stage. God uses adversity to move us from the first (immature) stage to the third (mature) stage.

Stage One: The Convenience Stage

The first stage of our spiritual life is salvation. This is the Convenience Stage. Our focus at this stage is on what God can do for us and the benefits that He showers on us by His grace. God calls us into a relationship with Him through His Son. We accept Christ into our lives because there is a direct benefit—salvation.

All who come to Christ begin at this stage. Many, unfortunately, never move beyond it. The problem with Stage One Christianity is that our intimacy with God is limited. Our commitment to Him is determined by whether or not it is convenient for us to obey Him. Our level of faith is weak and simplistic. God never intended that we should remain at such a primitive place in our relationship with Him.

Stage Two: The Crisis Stage

You may have heard the term "foxhole Christianity." There is something about a crisis that concentrates our minds on God. The problem with

Stage Two faith is that none of us can remain there. We must either go deeper into our relationship with God or we must go back. Unfortunately, all too many people return to the previous stage as soon as the crisis is over. What a tragedy to waste the lessons of adversity!

When God sends a crisis into our life, He wants us to desire *Him*, not just an escape from the problem. The psalmist wrote, "My heart says of you, 'Seek his face!' Your face, LORD, I will seek" (Ps. 27:8). God doesn't just want us to seek His hand. He wants us to seek His face. When we are in a crisis, we tend to seek His hand of deliverance. That's a "Help me, Lord!" attitude. But God wants us to go farther and deeper in our relationship with Him. That's what the next stage is all about.

Stage Three: Conviction Stage

God desires that we develop an intimate and obedient relationship with Him—a relationship motivated by love. In this stage, our attitude is no longer "Bless me, Lord," nor "Help me, Lord." It is "Have me, Lord." At this stage, the heart of the believer has been fully circumcised. The believer is humble and obedient. Former things have been removed. The circumcised heart is a new and different heart.

Job reached the Conviction Stage when he was able to say of God, "Though He slay me, yet will I trust Him" (Job 13:15, *NKJV*). Through Job's trial of adversity, God accomplished that deeper work He seeks to produce in your life and mine.

When we reach the Conviction Stage, we are no longer focused merely on being saved, blessed or rescued. At this stage, we begin to live the gospel of the Kingdom. We experience God as never before. It's a life often accompanied by miracles and answered prayer. We walk as Jesus walked. This is the place in which God wants every one of His children to be. As John wrote, "This is how we know we are in him: Whoever claims to live in him must walk as Jesus did" (1 John 2:5-6).

Every major character in the Bible went through these three stages. For example, Peter met Jesus on the seashore and chose to follow Him (Stage One). However, it was not until he faced his crisis of belief after denying Christ (Stage Two) that he was forced to decide what he really believed about Jesus. In that crisis, Satan sifted Peter as wheat, but Jesus prayed for Peter that his faith would not fail. That prayer carried Peter through his crisis stage and into the conviction stage (Stage Three), where God used him mightily in the Kingdom.

In the Lord's Prayer, Jesus prayed, "Thy kingdom come. Thy will be done in earth, as it is in heaven" (Matt. 6:10, *KJV*). Christians today focus far more on the transaction of becoming a Christian—on becoming born again—than on the kingdom of God. However, a careful examination of the Gospels reveals that Jesus taught far more about the kingdom of God than He taught about the transaction of salvation. Yes, salvation is the doorway to the Kingdom, but Jesus never intended for us to park ourselves in the doorway! He wants us to move on into the Kingdom.

Many evangelism programs train believers to share their faith, which is important. However, if we truly lived out the kingdom of God, the fruit of our lives would be the saving of many souls. If God's people authentically lived out the kingdom of God, we wouldn't have to develop evangelism programs. Our very lives would attract the unsaved.

Adversity That Reveals God's Faithfulness

Before my trial of adversity, whenever I heard of people going through financial failures, I'd look at them with a judgmental attitude. I thought their adversity was due to poor management of their resources. I prided myself on my own discipline as a manager and gave myself credit for my success.

Then my financial world crumbled to dust. What are the odds that two unrelated investments totaling $300,000 would fail almost simultaneously? Or that I would lose 70 percent of my income stream at the same time? Or that a longtime client would suddenly refuse to pay a bill of $140,000?

I had to cash in my IRAs just to pay living expenses and service my debts, which cost me a lot of money in penalties. At the same time, I was carrying two mortgages, a hefty child support and alimony payment, and a business that was no longer generating the income it once had. I was forced to trust God at a totally new level. Once I got to the bottom,

He began showing me His faithfulness in my finances.

Here's just one example among many: Soon after I met Gunnar Olson, he invited me to the 1997 Global Conference on World Evangelism in South Africa—a gathering of 4,000 Christians from 140 nations with a goal of reaching the world with the gospel of Jesus Christ. The conference featured a special "marketplace track" for 600 business leaders from around the world. I refused to charge the trip on my credit card. If I was going to go, God would have to provide.

The last day of registration came and I still had no money for the trip. I had given up on going when a man walked into my office and said, "You're supposed to go to that conference. Here is $2,500 for you to go." He had taken the money from his personal savings. I was overwhelmed by his generosity and by God's amazing provision.

I shouldn't have been surprised. That's exactly what God has promised to do. Paul was sitting in a prison in Rome, writing to suffering, persecuted Christians in Philippi, when he wrote: "And my God will meet all your needs according to his glorious riches in Christ Jesus" (Phil. 4:19).

At one point during the depths of my trial, God gave me a Scripture passage that seemed to be written specifically for me:

> Although the Lord gives you the bread of adversity and the water of affliction, your teachers will be hidden no more; with your own eyes you will see them. Whether you turn to the right or to the left, your ears will hear a voice behind you, saying, "This is the way; walk in it." Then you will defile your idols overlaid with silver and your images covered with gold; you will throw them away like a menstrual cloth and say to them, "Away with you!" He will also send you rain for the seed you sow in the ground, and the food that comes from the land will be rich and plentiful. In that day your cattle will graze in broad meadows (Isa. 30:20-23).

If we can't trust God in the tough times, when can we trust Him? "The LORD is close to the brokenhearted," wrote the psalmist, "and saves those who are crushed in spirit" (Ps. 34:18). No matter what you may be facing right now, God knows what you are going through—and you can rely on His faithfulness.

Adversity That Produces Holiness

For about six weeks after I separated from my first wife, my 12-year-old daughter was estranged from me. I could accept the fact that my wife had rejected me, but why did my daughter reject me as well? Baffled and drowning in hurt, I had to trust that God would somehow bring healing out of this situation.

One day, in the depths of my suffering, I sat down with two friends and poured out my pain to them. Their response surprised me.

"Os," one of them said, "I can see that you've accepted this situation as being from God. But stoic acceptance isn't what God is after. He wants you to have joy in this trial."

"Joy?" I said. "My marriage is over and my daughter has turned her back on me. I'm supposed to feel joy? Stoic acceptance is the best I can do right now."

"That's the problem," said my other friend. "You have the attitude of a survivalist. But unless you believe that God has the right to do these things in your life and accept this adversity with joy, you'll return to the way you were before this trial began."

Those were strong words—and my soul resisted them. But as I considered what my friends were telling me, I realized that they were right. I was persevering through my trials and even building character. But I had no joy. I was just what they said I was: a survivalist. I was operating in a suck-it-up mode.

James 1:2 tells us to consider it pure joy whenever we face trials of many kinds, but I was not rejoicing. I was just plodding through my trials, hoping to outlast them.

"So," I said to my two friends, "what am I supposed to do?"

Their answer: "You need to come to a place in which God is free to do anything He wants in your life. You still feel that you are entitled to certain things from God, but you're not. You aren't letting God be God."

That was a transforming moment in my Joseph Pit experience.

In the Early Church, believers understood that God had the right to do anything He wanted. They counted it a privilege to suffer in His name. But I saw suffering as an imposition, an injustice. I had the same attitude that afflicts most of American Christianity: I was seeking a God I *wanted*, not the God who *is*.

The God I wanted was a God who would respond immediately to my cries for help and deliver me from my suffering. But the God who *is* has already told us that Christians will suffer in this life and that adversity comes with the territory. He is the God who told us that His Son learned obedience through suffering (see Heb. 5:8). If Jesus had to learn obedience, why shouldn't we?

But we don't want to learn obedience! We want an obedient God. We want to be able to tell God in prayer, "Do this," and He will do it. We want a God we can command like the genie in Aladdin's lamp. We forget that the purpose of prayer is to align our will with God's, not to align His will with ours!

We Americans like to think that as citizens of God's kingdom, we live in a democracy. But the Kingdom is not a democracy; it's a monarchy. God is sovereign; we're not. In fact, we don't even get a vote. We are to obey, period.

During that difficult time of estrangement, I read Hannah Hurnard's allegory, *Hinds' Feet on High Places*. In this book, the author chronicles the journey of Much-Afraid, a woman who has been called by the Shepherd to scale the mountain of Love. Her companions on the long, difficult journey are Sorrow and Suffering. Much-Afraid's relatives—Craven Fear, Aunt Dismal Forebodings, Spiteful, Gloomy, Lord Fearing, Pride, Bitterness and Resentment, and Self-Pity—want Much-Afraid to stay and comfort them. But the Shepherd tells Much-Afraid that she must leave them behind in order to climb the mountain of Love.

At one point, the similarities between the story of Much-Afraid and my own journey were uncanny. The heights she had to scale were so much like the obstacles I faced:

Much-Afraid covered her face with her hands and sank down on a rock with a horror and dread in her heart such as she had never felt before. Then she felt her two companions take her hands in theirs and heard them say, "Do not be afraid, Much-Afraid, this is not a dead-end after all, and we shall not have to turn back. There is a way up the face of the precipice. The hart and the hind have shown it to us quite plainly. We shall be able to follow it too and make the ascent."

"Oh, no! No!" Much-Afraid almost shrieked. "That path is utterly impossible. The deer may be able to manage it, but no mere human being could."[1]

A hart, of course, is an adult male deer, and a hind is a female deer. As I read about the hart and the hind, I thought of my two friends who had gently confronted me about my need to accept adversity with joy. They were the hart and hind in my life, showing me the path of ascent that God wanted me to take. They reminded me of God's upward call on my life.

Yes, the trail of adversity seemed impossibly steep, and I kept encountering one obstacle after another that sent me sliding back down the mountain. The feeling of being rejected by my daughter was only the most recent in a series of obstacles. But my two friends were going before me, marking and clearing the path, making a seemingly impossible climb a bit easier.

My two friends were especially close to me on Father's Day. Although I received no note or phone call from my wife or daughter that day, my two friends spent time with me, helping me over a rocky part of the path.

Most important of all, my two friends didn't coddle me or patronize me. They told me what I *needed* to hear (even if it wasn't what I *wanted* to hear). They helped me see that I had to give up my right to my daughter. They helped me realize that if Abraham could trust God to raise a sacrificed son from the dead, then God could restore my "dead" relationship with my daughter. Eventually, there was healing in the relationship between me and my daughter. But even before the healing came, I experienced genuine acceptance with joy.

In the conclusion of Hannah Hurnard's allegory, Much-Afraid reaches the mountaintop. There, Shepherd transforms her feet into hinds' feet—which means that she can now mark the ascending path for others. The image of the hinds' feet, by the way, comes from Habakkuk 3:19—"The LORD God is my strength, and he will make my feet like hinds' feet, and he will make me to walk upon mine high places" (*KJV*).

Shepherd also gives her a new name: Grace and Glory. Then Shepherd asks her what she has learned. Grace and Glory replies that she has learned the following lessons: First, when trials come, she must accept those trials with joy. Second, when mistreated, she must forgive without bitterness so that Shepherd can bring good out of evil. Third, Shepherd never saw her as she was—lame, weak and cowardly—but as she would be when she reached the mountaintop. Fourth, everything that happens, no matter how tragic, will be transformed into beauty if she responds in obedience.

Shepherd tells her that she has learned well. The lessons she has learned have transformed her from crippled Much-Afraid to beautiful Grace and Glory, a creature who leaps on the mountaintops with hinds' feet. The Shepherd tells her that if she obeys the Law of Love, nothing will be able to cripple her hinds' feet or separate her from Him. He tells her that this is the secret of the High Places. It is the lovely and perfect law of the entire universe.

Weeks later, a close friend and I were talking about the events that had occurred over the past few months in my life. "Os," he said, "I don't understand why you're having to go through this. I just can't see the positives in all the adversity you're going through."

I thought about it and then said, "I can see many blessings in my adversity. Let me list some for you. First, I believe God allowed me to experience financial loss as a loving reproof from Him. Because of strongholds of insecurity and fear, I had allowed money to become an idol, my source of security. God loved me enough to correct me and pull me back to Him.

"Second, I can see that God is using adversity to prepare me for ministry to others. God is a complex strategic thinker. He can accomplish a variety of goals with just one event. He's going to use my adversity not just for my benefit, but also to help others.

"Third, I can see that God is preparing me for a ministry with businesspeople. I've already encountered a number of men who are experiencing problems in their businesses and in their marriages. It's no accident that all of these men are crossing my path. I've been able to help them see that God uses the imperfections of their mates to make them more Christlike. And I've been able to help them see that God is the source of all blessings, including the success they take credit for."

As I look around the marketplace, I see many Christian business-people who have not yet arrived in the Promised Land of God's king-dom. They are still living in Egypt among the gods of greed and pleasure. They want to reflect Christ in their careers, but they're blinded by the values of this culture. They see their businesses as theirs, not God's. I don't blame them—I once viewed life the same way.

Today, like the apostle Paul, I'm able to say, "I know what it is to be in need, and I know what it is to have plenty" (Phil. 4:12). Yet I am hum-bled when I recall that Paul wrote those words from a cold, filthy prison cell. I have gone through adversity, but not one-hundredth of the adver-sity that Paul went through, and not one-millionth of the adversity that Jesus suffered when He nailed my sins to the cross. So I count it a bless-ing, not a burden, to have gone through some measure of suffering so that God could mold me into the man He wants me to be.

Many are the blessings that come from adversity—and I wouldn't trade them for all the wealth in the world.

QUESTIONS FOR REFLECTION

1. Has God ever used you to help someone who was going through trials? Did that experience change the way you looked at your own trials of adversity?

2. In your Christian walk, are you at Stage One: Convenience ("Bless me, Lord!"), Stage Two: Crisis ("Help me, Lord!") or Stage Three: Conviction ("Have me, Lord!")? Explain your answer with examples from your experience.

3. What needs to change in your life in order for you to come to the third stage?

4. As you live in relationship to God right now, are you seeking His hand or seeking His face? Explain.

5. Are you able to trust that God will bring good out of everything that happens in your life, including tragedy and calamity? If not, why not?

6. What are three blessings that God has brought out of your trial of adversity? If you can't think of any, ask a close friend to pray that God would reveal those blessings to you.

Note

1. Hannah Hurnard, *Hinds' Feet on High Places* (Wheaton, IL: Tyndale Publishing House, 1986), pp. 121-122.

13

CONFRONTING THE FEAR OF FAILURE

Forgetting what is behind and straining toward what is ahead,
I press on toward the goal to win the prize for which God has
called me heavenward in Christ Jesus.

PHILIPPIANS 3:13-14

When I was 16, I was an accomplished junior golfer. I had played in many tournaments throughout my home state as well as in the United States Junior Amateur. My goal in life was to play professional golf.

At one point, I participated in a state-level tournament and was favored to win. However, although I played well early on, I choked in the last round and ended up well behind the leaders. I was devastated.

I came home and broke down in front of my mother. She consoled me, which is what mothers do. I realize now that I didn't really need a mother's tender consolation. I needed a hard-nosed coach to yank me out of my trough of self-pity and say, "Every competitor goes through failure! Learn a lesson from it and keep going!"

Because I didn't have that kind of coaching, I didn't know that getting nervous and tense during a competition was a common affliction in competitive sports. I didn't know that I could overcome it. Instead, that one failure made me see myself as a failure—someone who couldn't handle the heat of competition.

I played in other tournaments and often jumped out to an early lead, only to tighten up and fall back in the pack as the pressure mounted. My self-esteem was based on my performance—and I was performing terribly! I went on to land a scholarship and become a club professional for three years, but I never fulfilled my potential as a golfer.

Years later, I learned to loosen up, have fun and let go of the tension—and I won a local club championship. If I had learned that lesson earlier in life, who knows how far I might have gone as a golfer.

Failure hurts. Whether you fail in marriage, business or golf, failure undermines your self-esteem as few other experiences can. But failure isn't the final word on your life. It's just one of the raw ingredients God uses to manufacture success.

Learning the Lessons of Failure

Back in the 1970s, Tom Watson was the up and coming golfer on the PGA Tour. But time after time, when Tom led a tournament coming into the last round, he would choke, bogey a few holes, and finish in the middle of the pack. Soon, the media began calling him a "choker." That kind of criticism only increases the pressure and the tendency to choke.

In an interview with Guy Yocom for *Golf Digest*, Watson said, "Everybody has choked. In the 1974 U.S. Open, I kept hitting the ball right to right. My nerves wouldn't allow me to adjust. That's what choking is—being so nervous you can't find a swing or a putting stroke you can trust."[1]

How did Watson overcome his tendency to choke? "Byron gave me the best cure for it," Watson recalled, referring to Byron Nelson, the legendary golf pro of the 1930s and '40s. "[Byron said], 'Walk slowly, talk slowly, deliberately do everything more slowly than you normally do. It has a way of settling you down.'"[2] That advice helped Tom Watson overcome his nervousness. He went on to win many tournaments, including five British Opens.

"Success," said Winston Churchill, "is going from failure to failure without loss of enthusiasm." Everybody fails. It's part of the process that leads us to maturity and success. Most successful entrepreneurs have been through a number of failures in life, but they usually don't think of their failures as defeats. They think of them as lessons.

God uses broken things and broken people to accomplish His plans. When David was anointed to be the future king of Israel, he was just a boy, the youngest of all the sons of Jesse. Later, David married Michal, the daughter of King Saul, and became a close friend of Saul's son Jonathan. King Saul had already lost the anointing of God and knew that David was destined to take his place. Fearful and jealous, Saul plotted to kill David, forcing the future king to flee to the hills.

As David hid from King Saul, he must have wondered, *Why am I living as a fugitive? I'm the next king of Israel!* He was a hunted man. His cause looked like a failure. Then something interesting happened: David began to attract other "failures" to his cause.

The Scriptures tell us, "All those who were in distress or in debt or discontented gathered around him, and he became their leader" (1 Sam. 22:2). David became the leader of a rag-tag band of failures—people whose lives were in chaos and who had experienced financial failure. They became David's army, known throughout the world as the greatest ever assembled. However, they weren't great because of their successes; they were great because God was behind them. The Lord turned David's band of failures into mighty men of valor (see 1 Chron. 11:10; 28:1).

If you hope to succeed, learn everything you can from your failures. In *The Three Success Secrets of Shamgar*, Orlando Magic executive Pat Williams observed, "Our experiences may not all be triumphs and successes, but so what? Failure is usually a far better teacher than success—if we are willing to learn the lessons. As Houston Astros pitcher Larry Dierker observed, 'Experience is the best teacher, but a hard grader. She gives the test first, the lesson later.'"[3]

Don't Let Fear Hold You Back

In our culture, we treat failure as a reason for disqualification. *God sees failure as preparation for success.* We need to stop looking at failure as the world sees it and start looking at failure from God's perspective.

God never gets mired in the past. He is constantly acting, creating and innovating. "See, I am doing a new thing! Now it springs up; do you not perceive it? I am making a way in the desert and streams in the wasteland" (Isa. 43:19). Someone once said, "When your memories are bigger than your dreams, you're headed for the grave." God wants to give us new dreams that are bigger than anything that has ever happened to us in the past.

God is daily giving us a fresh revelation of His purpose for our lives. Are we listening? He wants us to live with a sense of excitement and enthusiasm and a willingness to dare great things in His name. He wants to transform the desert wastelands of our past into a lush green Eden flowing with streams of life-giving water. Are we ready to receive the new thing He has prepared for us?

When I met Angie, we began having serious discussions about marriage after we had only been dating for a few months. I had already spent 14 years in a difficult marriage that had ended in a painful divorce. Fortunately, I had also gone through several years of healing in which God had rebuilt my ability to trust. My reliance on God overshadowed my fear of failure. God gave me a second chance at a successful marriage. Angie has been God's gift of grace in my life.

After eight years of marriage, Angie and I have never been more in love. Have we had challenges and setbacks? You bet we have. But Angie and I work on our problems, solve them in reliance upon God, and grow closer with each new challenge. I'm so glad that I didn't let the fear of failure keep me from experiencing a lifetime of joy.

After an experience of failure, it's understandable that we might be afraid to take another risk. But fear is no excuse. God expects us to follow His plan for our lives in spite of our fears. He expects us to dare great things in His name, trusting that He will never let us fall. As the psalmist writes:

I lift up my eyes to the hills—
    where does my help come from?
My help comes from the LORD,
    the Maker of heaven and earth.
He will not let your foot slip—
    he who watches over you will not slumber (Ps. 121:1-3).

I've met many people who have a lot of talent, wonderful gifts and great ideas but who are accomplishing little or nothing. Why? Because they are afraid of making a mistake! They're ruled by a mentality of perfectionism. Everything must be just-so before they will attempt something big. They fear that if they step out in faith, God won't be there to meet them. So they stay where there's no risk—and no chance of achieving anything of value. Or, they go to the other extreme: They sabotage success, subconsciously thinking that they don't deserve it.

When I began writing *TGIF*, my daily e-mail devotional, I was concerned about my grammar skills. In those days, I didn't have the resources to hire an editor, so I would write one message a day, send it off from my computer, and trust that God would use it in the lives of my subscribers despite my occasional mangling of the English language. I soon began receiving such comments as, "Os, I really love your messages each day. But have you ever thought of hiring an editor?"

Yes, I'd thought of it—but I couldn't afford it. Finally, after receiving a number of these gentle suggestions, I responded to one by saying, "Would you like the job?" The person turned out to be an English teacher living in Hong Kong. He said, "Yes, I'd love to." That's how I acquired my first editor. And he did it for free! Today, *TGIF* is read by hundreds of thousands of people every day, but it never would have happened if I had let the fear of failure or the fear of what others think rule my life.

"There Is a Shaking Coming"

Louisiana businessman Bill Hamm is a friend of mine—and a contemporary Joseph. Bill co-owned and ran his family's contracting business, and was accustomed to success. He masterminded a new heavy industrial division in the mid-1980s that became the mainstay of his family's firm.

Bill entered his Joseph Pit experience in 1999. The first hint that he was about to undergo such an experience came when his friend John told him, "Bill, the Lord gave me a word in my quiet time this morning for you: 'I am calling you out to count for the Kingdom and to do great things in the Kingdom. There is a shaking coming.'"

Bill considered those words. Being called out to do great things for the Kingdom sounded good, but what did God mean about a shaking? That didn't sound good at all! It didn't fit Bill's paradigm about God, which said that if you live faithfully and righteously, God will bless you. Bill lived a decent life. He didn't drink, smoke or curse. He had become the youngest deacon at his 6,000-member church. He'd taught Sunday School. Everyone thought that Bill Hamm was a model Christian.

But deep inside, Bill knew that he didn't have a living relationship with the Lord. He hungered for something more than just religion. He wanted a deeper relationship with God. Yet that word from the Lord troubled him. Although he didn't know what it might mean, he knew that he didn't want to go through a shaking. But six months after John shared that prophetic word with Bill, the shaking began.

The year 1999 started with a bang. Bill's new division was an astounding success. The company's revenue jumped from $38 million to $64 million. But after that auspicious beginning, bad things began to happen. As the year ended, three major projects showed huge losses. Even with the increased revenues, the company finished $7 million in the red. It was not unusual for one big job to go south, but three at the same time? That had never happened before. It placed the entire company in jeopardy.

A series of lengthy, costly lawsuits consumed the next three years of Bill's life and cost his company a million dollars in legal fees. The stress drove him into a severe depression. Yet even though Bill couldn't understand what God was doing through this time of shaking, he knew that his only hope was to hang on to God for dear life.

Bill's Joseph Pit experience brought him to the end of himself. He learned the meaning of Psalm 126:5: "Those who sow in tears will reap with songs of joy." He recalls, "I used those three years to 'sow in tears.' Eventually, just as God restored Joseph, He restored me and made me fruitful in the land of my suffering."

Finally, Bill felt God prompting him to sell off the division he had developed. God's timing was amazing: An offer to buy the division came in just three hours before a meeting with the bank was scheduled to put the company into the bank's Special Assets and Collections Department.

Bill decided to dedicate the business to the Lord and run it purely on biblical principles. His uncle, who was half-owner of the company, didn't share Bill's vision. Once the company recovered financially, the uncle pushed Bill out of the business. Bill felt betrayed, but he soon realized that God was using this adversity in his life to bring about his complete surrender to the Lord.

A few days after leaving the business, Bill was on a friend's boat in Arkansas. His friend told him about a new energy technology with phenomenal possibilities. He wanted Bill's help in bringing it to market. It was an idea that God had given to this man during his prayer time—"a world-changing technology," Bill said.

Again, the timing was perfect. Just a few weeks earlier, Bill had been at a conference in which a speaker had said that the Lord was unleashing "witty inventions" upon the world. This phrase comes from a verse in Proverbs that in the *King James Version* reads, "I wisdom dwell with prudence, and find out knowledge of witty inventions" (8:12). Bill was convinced that God in His wisdom would give creative concepts and ideas ("witty inventions") to people, and that this energy innovation was one of them.

So Bill became involved in an effort to bring this invention to a worldwide market. He set up a team of 21 intercessors to establish a prayer foundation for the business. They prayed for a year and a half before putting the formation documents in place. As the company transitioned to the implementation phase, these intercessors became a spiritual board of directors.

Today, the five startup partners in Bill Hamm's company see their business as *more* than a business. They intend to build the principles of heaven into the company's business model, making it an example for all Christian businesses to emulate. And they expect the company to generate massive returns that will be used to advance God's kingdom and bless people around the world. As they see it, God has made them stewards of this innovative technology. Bill Hamm is looking forward to seeing how God will use this venture to advance His purposes in the world.

This story is a work-in-progress. The invention is not yet on the market. There have been delays and obstacles, and Bill accepts these problems as tests of his willingness to wait upon the Lord. It's a lot different from the usual Christian approach to business, whereby people devise a business plan and then ask God to rubber-stamp it. "Under this business model," Bill says, "we aren't the owners of this company. We're stewards. God owns it, and our spiritual board of directors helps us maintain that focus."

Bill Hamm is grateful for his experience of failure, because that's what it took for God to move him from being a mere pew-warmer to being a true steward of His treasury of wealth and ideas. "Failure brings you to the point of surrender," Bill says. "Most of us aren't ready to surrender until we reach a point of desperation. That's where God had to take me. It hurt. It broke my ego. It shattered my dreams. But that failure is paying rich dividends today. Today I know God in a way I never knew Him before—and that makes it all worthwhile."

Peace: Our Weapon Against Fear

We know that God doesn't want us to live in fear. As the apostle Paul wrote to his spiritual son Timothy, "For God did not give us a spirit of timidity, but a spirit of power, of love and of self-discipline" (2 Tim. 1:7).

Fear is the enemy of faith. Fear is bondage. Satan wants us to live in bondage to the past, but God wants us to live in the freedom of His love and power. As Paul wrote, "For you did not receive a spirit that makes you a slave again to fear, but you received the Spirit of sonship. And by him we cry, 'Abba, Father'" (Rom. 8:15).

In order to be the leaders God calls us to be, we must conquer our fear and put it to death. This is a spiritual battle, and it can only be won with spiritual weapons. We must replace our fear with the peace that passes understanding. As Jesus told His followers, "I have told you these things, so that in me you may have peace. In this world you will have trouble. But take heart! I have overcome the world" (John 16:33).

What is this peace the Lord speaks of? In his book *The Three Battlegrounds*, my friend Francis Frangipane tells us:

Our peace does not come from extreme indifference, nor is it from becoming so "spiritual" that you fail to notice a problem.

Thirteen Lessons I Have Learned from Past Failures

1. Going through failure doesn't make me a failure. It's simply one step in a process of improvement that leads to success.

2. Going through failure reveals strengths and weaknesses in myself that I never would have discovered otherwise.

3. Failure is not the tragedy I once thought it was. Failure is a normal part of life.

4. If you view past failures with the right attitude, you gain wisdom that you can apply to build a successful future.

5. My failures have taught me to accept others who have failed and to identify with their struggles.

6. I have learned that almost all successful people have failed in the past. They use the lessons of failure as stepping-stones to success.

7. I have learned not to let fear of failure prevent me from daring great things with God.

8. I have discovered that God is faithful and will provide for my needs.

9. I have learned that playing it safe and avoiding risks are sure prescriptions for failure.

10. Through my experience with failure, I have gained relationships with people I never would have met otherwise.

11. Through failure, I have learned to overcome my shyness and introvert personality. I am a public speaker today because I have gone through the crucible of failure.

12. Because of past failures, I now have a wife who daily shows me what a successful marriage relationship can be.

13. Through failure, I have learned that God's strength is perfected in weakness. This is how He is able to use me for His purposes.

It is being so confident in God's love that you know, regardless of the battle and the difficulties in your circumstances, that "greater is He who is in you than he who is in the world" (see 1 John 4:4). You are not self-assured, you are God-assured.[4]

That's the confidence and assurance we need to overcome our fears and risk great things for the Kingdom. That's the peace we need to cast out our fear of failure. As the apostle Paul told the persecuted Christians in Rome, "The God of peace will soon crush Satan under your feet" (Rom. 16:20). The God of peace is our conquering King; the peace of God is our weapon against fear and Satan. Before going to the cross, Jesus told His disciples, "Peace I leave with you; my peace I give you. I do not give to you as the world gives. Do not let your hearts be troubled and do not be afraid" (John 14:27).

In Mark 4, we read the story of Jesus and His disciples crossing the lake in a fishing boat. Along the way, Jesus fell asleep. As He slept, a storm arose and the waves beat against the boat, swamping it with water. The Lord's disciples feared for their lives, but Jesus continued to sleep. Finally, they woke Him and cried out, "Teacher, don't You care that we're about to perish?"

Jesus got up, went to the side of the boat, and said, "Peace. Be still." Instantly, the wind died to less than a whisper and the water became calm and smooth.

I suspect that Jesus was speaking as much to His fearful disciples as He was to the wind and waves when He said, "Peace. Be still." And He was speaking to our fears as well. His word to us in the storms of life is, "Peace. Be still. Why are you so fearful? Why do you lack the faith to risk everything for My kingdom? Why don't you trust Me in the storms of your life?"

Fear is a *natural* response to obstacles, adversity and failure, but peace is the *supernatural* response that God gives us by His grace. Just as Jesus had authority over the wind and waves, He has authority over the storms in our lives. He has authority over our doubts, fears and shame. These are the weapons of Satan, but Jesus stands against Satan's fury and says with authority, "Peace. Be still." The peace of God shatters the weapons of Satan and sends our enemy fleeing.

On the evening of the first Easter, the disciples were gathered in a house in Jerusalem. They had the doors locked, because they were afraid that the religious leaders who had crucified their Lord would be coming for them as well. The disciples were filled with fear and shame. They had failed Jesus and forsaken Him in His hour of need.

This was their Joseph Pit. Their dream of reigning with Jesus in His kingdom had been crucified along with their Master. It looked as if Satan had won. Now there was nothing left but a black hole of regret and despair.

Then, in the midst of the darkness, Jesus appeared. He walked through the locked doors of their fear and stood among them. And the first words He spoke to them were "peace be with you."

Peace!

If ever a group of people needed the peace of God in their hearts, they did. The instant the disciples heard Jesus speak the word "peace," their fear melted away. They were filled with joy as Christ showed them His pierced hands and side.

Then, once more, Jesus said to them, "Peace be with you! As the Father has sent me, I am sending you" (John 20:21). Then He breathed on them and said, "Receive the Holy Spirit" (v. 22).

What Jesus did for His disheartened followers on that first Easter He still does for you and me today. He arms us with His peace and sends us out into the world to claim this planet for His kingdom. Most important of all, He imparts the Holy Spirit to us.

It is the Spirit who produces fruit in our lives. As the apostle Paul tells us, "But the fruit of the Spirit is love, joy, peace, patience, kindness, goodness, faithfulness, gentleness and self-control. Against such things there is no law" (Gal. 5:22-23). I believe that the fruit of the Spirit listed in this passage forms a progression in our lives. It starts with love—the love of God and others. As we love, we experience joy. That joy produces greater peace, which then yields patience, kindness, goodness, faithfulness, gentleness and self-control.

But how do we overcome our fears—including the fear of failure—so that we can experience God's peace in stormy, turbulent times? The apostle Paul explains:

Do not be anxious about anything, but in everything, by prayer and petition, with thanksgiving, present your requests to God. And the peace of God, which transcends all understanding, will guard your hearts and your minds in Christ Jesus. Finally, brothers, whatever is true, whatever is noble, whatever is right, whatever is pure, whatever is lovely, whatever is admirable— if anything is excellent or praiseworthy—think about such things. Whatever you have learned or received or heard from me, or seen in me—put it into practice. And the God of peace will be with you (Phil. 4:6-9).

So, if we want to have peace, we must present our requests to God and give thanks to God. But what does that mean? Should we say, "Thank You, God, for my marriage troubles"? or "Thank You, God, for my cancer"? or "Thank You, God, for my bankruptcy"?

I don't think that's what Paul is saying. I believe we are to thank God for being *God.* I believe we are to thank Him for being all-powerful, for being loving, for being present in our adversity, for being close to us in our pain, for identifying with us through His Son, for being in control of all of our circumstances. God asks us to do what is *unnatural* (praise Him in the midst of adversity) so that He can do something *supernatural* (give us peace in the midst of the storm).

Moreover, Paul tells us to keep our thoughts and emotions focused on the positive—on things that are true, noble, right, pure, lovely, admirable, excellent and praiseworthy. If we do that, he says, the God of peace will be with us.

We can have peace in the midst of pain. We can have peace in the midst of adversity. We can have peace in the midst of failure, because the God of peace has sent the Prince of Peace to be our Lord, our Savior, and our Example.

In the Garden of Gethsemane, in the shadow of the cross, Jesus experienced the most awful anguish that any human being has ever endured. The horror He faced was so great that He sweat drops of blood. Yet He experienced such a supernatural peace that He was able to face the terrors of the cross with the words, "Not my will, but yours be done" (Luke 22:42).

This same peace is available to us today. No matter how we have failed in the past, the God of peace is leading us to success. Satan tries to terrorize us, but God shatters the weapons of Satan and then calls us to freedom and a bold adventure.

The peace of God is our ultimate weapon against fear.

QUESTIONS FOR REFLECTION

1. Think of a time when you experienced failure. How did you respond? Did you put your failure behind you? Did you let it paralyze you?

2. Name at least three lessons you have learned from your past failures. Have you relied on past successes or failures to dictate what you will do in the future? Explain your answer.

3. Describe at least one false notion that you had about failure before reading this chapter. What is the most practical or helpful insight you've learned about failure from this chapter?

4. What is your greatest fear? How has fear hindered your life? What practical steps can you take to resolve and conquer your fear?

5. Do you experience the peace of God? If not, what hinders you?

Notes

1. Tom Watson, "My Shot: Tom Watson," interview by Guy Yocom, *Golf Digest*, July 2004. http://www.golfdigest.com/majors/britishopen/index.ssf?/majors/britishopen/gd200 407myshot.html (accessed May 2006).
2. Ibid.
3. Pat Williams and Jay Strack, *The Three Success Secrets of Shamgar* (Deerfield Beach, FL: Health Communications, Inc., 2004), p. 103.
4. Francis Frangipane, *The Three Battlegrounds* (Cedar Rapids, IA: Arrow Publications, 1989), p. 71-72.

DARE TO FULFILL YOUR JOSEPH CALLING

*With this in mind, we constantly pray for you, that our God may count
you worthy of his calling, and that by his power he may fulfill every good
purpose of yours and every act prompted by your faith.*

2 THESSALONIANS 1:11

During my flight in 1997 to the Global Conference on World Evangelism,
I overheard two men talking in the row ahead of me. They were also going
to the conference, so I introduced myself. One of the men was Morris
Ruddick, a businessman from Denver. He was going to make a presenta-
tion to the business track at the conference. That day, Morris and I became
friends. A few years later, I had him speak at a conference I hosted.

Morris is an author, minister, United States Marine (retired) and an
entrepreneur with a mission of bringing ministries and businesses
together to serve God and meet human need. He has a special burden for
assisting Christian believers in Israel and in lands where there is persecution, political upheaval or natural disasters.

Morris's own journey has taken him through a season of intense
adversity and painful loss. In late 1996, his 30-year-old daughter was
murdered. The traumatic loss challenged everything he stood for and
forced him to re-examine his life. The loss of his daughter became, as he
says, "a paradigm shift second only to my salvation experience."

Morris also experienced a series of crises in his business life. He felt strongly led by the Lord to start a consulting business and quickly built up a clientele of Fortune 500 companies and ministry organizations. His consulting business expanded rapidly, opening offices in Tulsa, Houston, Chicago and New York. Without warning, the markets he specialized in started to dry up. He closed offices, reduced staff, and then finally had to close down the company.

Morris wondered why God allowed his company to experience such rapid growth only to have it suddenly wither away. He had dedicated the company to God, and he envisioned it as a business that would bless and minister to people. One morning while he was praying and grieving the loss of his company, he felt the Lord speaking to him. "Morris," God told him, "My purpose for the company was the work I was doing in you." It was a stunning revelation: God was far more interested in *what he was* than in *what he did.*

Morris took a position as senior vice-president of a billion-dollar corporation. He had a vision of claiming that organization for God. At the same time, there were others in the organization who literally claimed it for Satan. They were part of a witchcraft coven, and they viewed the company as a seat of power. "At that juncture in my walk with the Lord, I had a fairly robust anointing as a prayer warrior," Morris recalled in his book *God's Economy, Israel and the Nations.* "But the spiritual backlash I began encountering definitely challenged and humbled me."[1]

Despite this spiritual opposition, Morris persevered in mobilizing Christians to be witnesses in the workplace. He led Bible studies and prayer groups in an office that belonged to the chairman of the board. But just as he was seeing God beginning to do a great work in that company, he was forced out.

Morris spent a long time seeking God's will for his life. He felt, in his words, "battered and confused." Morris had twice reached a point in which it seemed God was working in a mighty way—first in the company he'd founded and then in the company where he was employed—only to have everything collapse. How could he be effective for God if he had to keep starting over from scratch?

Finally, Morris realized that the Lord had a plan for his life that he never imagined. He sensed God telling him that he was going to have a ministry much like the ministries of Joseph and Daniel—two Old Testament leaders who went through great adversity as preparation for important roles on the world stage. God used Joseph to advance His kingdom purposes through a leadership position in Egypt. God used Daniel to advance His kingdom purposes through a leadership position in Babylon. And God was going to use Morris Ruddick to advance His kingdom purposes through a leadership position in the secular world marketplace of the twenty-first century.

Today, Morris Ruddick oversees the Strategic Global Intercession Network (www.strategicintercession.org), an Internet ministry that encourages intercessors, pastors, ministry leaders and business leaders to pray and become involved in projects that combine business and Christian ministry. He is also working to mobilize the evangelical church to stand with the nation of Israel against the growing forces of anti-Semitism in the world. Through his international consulting firm, The Ruddick International Group (http://ruddickintl.com/), Morris assists businesses and government entities in making fact-based plans and projections that help generate wealth and improve the lives of millions around the world.

Morris Ruddick is a modern-day Joseph who is encouraging an entire generation of modern-day Josephs to step forward and make a stand for the Kingdom in the workplace and the marketplace. Morris says that a "Joseph" is a person who

- hears God's voice and is spiritually in tune with the Lord
- is recognized as one on whom God's favor rests
- speaks the truth boldly, honestly and without fear or equivocation
- has a clear perception of life and operates from God's perspective
- is not limited by manmade tradition, but thinks creatively and innovatively
- understands the times

- is a humble servant-leader
- puts obedience to God's calling ahead of personal wants and desires
- looks to forge strategic alliances in the unlikeliest of places
- spends large amounts of time in the presence of the Lord
- does ministry out in the world's system, not in the religious cloister
- is a mover and shaker in the world of finance, business or government
- underwent preparation through a painful Joseph Pit experience

Morris Ruddick dares to obey God and fulfill his Joseph Calling—and he also challenges other believers to discover and fulfill their Joseph Calling. He has become a mentor to me and to countless other believers who are claiming the world for the kingdom of God.

The Dream and the Reality

Often our suffering seems to make no sense. Yet those are the times when God is truly at work behind the scenes, fulfilling His plan for our lives. This truth is vividly illustrated in the biblical story of Esther and Mordecai.

The story opens in the kingdom of Persia, modern-day Iran. At that time, the kingdom stretched from Africa to India and was ruled by King Xerxes, also known as Ahasuerus. After King Xerxes angrily banishes his Persian queen, Vashti, he selects a new queen—a beautiful young Jewish woman named Esther.

Orphaned at an early age, Esther was raised by her older cousin, Mordecai, an advisor to King Xerxes. Because the Jews were hated by the Persians, Mordecai instructs Esther to keep her Jewish ethnicity a secret.

Unfortunately, Mordecai makes an enemy of the Persian prime minister, an arrogant man named Haman, who then decides to rid himself of Mordecai and exterminate Mordecai's people, the Jews. Haman convinces King Xerxes to issue an order of genocide against the Jewish people and has a tall gallows constructed for Mordecai's execution. (At this point, neither Haman nor King Xerxes knows that Queen Esther is Jewish.)

When Mordecai learns of Haman's plot, he urges Queen Esther to go to the king and plead for the Jewish people. Although Esther is queen, Mordecai is asking her to risk her life. Under Persian law, no one may enter the king's presence uninvited, not even the queen. If Esther approaches the king and he is displeased, he can have her executed. Yet Queen Esther agrees to take the risk, saying, "I will go to the king, even though it is against the law. And if I perish, I perish" (Esther 4:16).

With fear and trembling, Esther enters the presence of King Xerxes. Fortunately, the king is pleased with her, and he promises to give her anything she asks for, up to half of his kingdom. In the end, King Xerxes issues an order of protection for the Jewish people—and has Haman executed on the gallows. The Jewish people are saved, and Mordecai is promoted to viceroy, the second-most powerful man in Persia.

There are several fascinating aspects of this story. First, nowhere in the book of Esther is God ever mentioned or even alluded to. Doesn't that seem odd? Yet God's *unseen* hand is truly everywhere, controlling events and protecting Esther, Mordecai and the Jewish people. Mordecai vaguely hints at God's unseen hand when he urges Esther to risk her life: "And who knows but that you have come to royal position for such a time as this?" (v. 14). Although Mordecai does not mention God by name, he clearly believes in a divine purpose working behind the scenes of history.

I think God has a reason for including a book in His Word in which His name isn't mentioned. He wants us to know that His unseen hand is with us, controlling events and protecting us, even when He seems silent and invisible. There are times when we think God has forgotten us and doesn't care about us. Yet He is always working in our lives, and no power in heaven or on Earth can derail His plans.

When we are in the place Hosea called the Valley of Achor (the Valley of Trouble), we can't see God's hand. We see nothing but opposition, obstacles and adversity. But God is working invisibly to turn our Valley of Achor into a door of hope.

A second fascinating aspect of this story is that there are many parallels between the story of Esther and Mordecai and the Joseph Calling. Both Esther and Mordecai had Joseph-like roles to play. Both faced death in order to save the Jewish people. Both achieved positions second only to the king—Esther had the royal position of the king's favored queen; Mordecai gained the political position of the king's viceroy.

A third interesting aspect is the role of obedience in Esther and Mordecai's lives. Both Esther and Mordecai had to become obedient to the point of death in order for God to intervene on their behalf. They had to dare to fulfill their Joseph calling. Only when they risked everything did God perform a miracle of deliverance.

Our lives are framed by the events and experiences that God takes us through, and our lives are defined by how we respond. Will we obey Him and dare great things for Him? Or will we shrink back in fear, denying our God-appointed destiny?

Adversity Is the Prerequisite to Destiny

I vividly recall what one man of God said to me while I was in the depths of my Joseph Pit experience. This man, who had gone through fiery testing, said, "You are a blessed man. God does not allow a man to be tested as you have been unless He has a special purpose planned for you." Although I didn't feel blessed by the adversity I was undergoing, his words were a great encouragement to me.

After two years of adversity, I began to catch glimpses of how God was working together the events of my life. I gradually began to understand why it was necessary for me to go through trials as preparation for His calling. I realized that, just as that godly man had told me, I was truly blessed to have been tested by God.

In the book of Job, the godly Job suffered loss and pain and then had to endure the unjust accusations of three "miserable comforters." Finally, a fourth man, wise young Elihu, says to Job, *"But those who suffer [God] delivers in their suffering; he speaks to them in their affliction"* (36:15).

During my Joseph Pit process, God sent a number of people to speak to me and encourage me in my affliction. I was grateful for the prophetic words and the glimpses of my future that God revealed to me from time to time. He used a number of unusual situations and spiritually wise people to let me know that He was using my pain for a unique Kingdom purpose.

We often cannot see what God has been doing in the valleys of life until we get up on the mountain. Only by looking back into the Valley of Achor, the Valley of Trouble, can we truly understand what God has taken us through—and why. As the Danish philosopher Soren Kierkegaard wrote in his journal in 1843, "Life can only be understood backwards, but it must be lived forwards."

I entered the Valley of Achor in March 1994 when my wife told me she wanted to end our marriage. Seven years later, I walked out of the Valley of Achor and passed through the door of hope—and God restored all that I had lost. He restored my finances through the sale of some property that I had kept throughout my Joseph Pit trial. The proceeds allowed me to pay all my creditors and become debt-free. God also restored my relationship with my daughter. Today, she is a strong Christian leader in her own right.

Next, in 1998 God brought Angie into my life. We were married nine months later. Through Angie's love and understanding, God has brought great healing to my life.

It amazes me that my trial of adversity lasted exactly seven years to the month. Seven years is the biblical number for completion. God made the world in six days and rested on the seventh. Egypt under Joseph experienced seven years of abundance followed by seven years of famine. God told Joshua to have seven priests blow seven trumpets on the seventh day while the people marched around Jericho seven times, and then the city walls fell. In the book of Revelation, there are seven lampstands, seven churches, seven years of tribulation, seven seals, seven trumpets and seven bowls of wrath.

I believe God gave me a message through those seven years of trial. God set aside seven special years of my life in order to prepare me and make me complete for the ministry He had planned for me. During those seven years, there were times I didn't want to live another day. Yet I could sense God saying, "Trust Me, Os. I'm not taking you through this pain merely to watch you suffer. In time, you'll understand."

Through this adversity, God birthed a new calling in my life. That calling involved a leadership role in the Faith At Work movement, a speaking ministry and a writing ministry—none of which I could have foreseen. I've traveled to 25 countries and shared this message of hope before hundreds of thousands of people. God truly turned my Valley of Achor into a door of hope. The Valley of Achor made me who I am today. God could not have used the man I was in the same way He is using the man I am.

In recent years, I have come to know a young man named Bradley Stuart. Bradley was born in South Africa with cerebral palsy and barely survived his birth. He did not walk until he was four. One of Bradley's legs was longer than the other, and he couldn't speak well. For most of his life, he has had little control over his shaking hands. In school, he was shunned and mistreated by his classmates. He grew up feeling bitter and angry.

When Bradley was 17, his father took him to a Christian healing service. Later that night, the boy's stunted leg miraculously grew two inches longer. When he awoke, he no longer walked with a limp. As a result, Bradley met the Savior and developed an intimate walk with Jesus. Today, he travels the world as an internationally known intercessor and the founder of a school of prayer. He has spoken hundreds of hours of knowledge to people in need of God's comfort and direction. God has used Bradley several times to help me discern His will for my life.

One evening in 1997, Bradley stood up in a meeting of about 40 workplace believers and handed a note to the leader. "This note is for someone here," Bradley said, "but I don't know who." I was on the last day of a 40-day fast and was seeking a revelation from God. When the leader read the message aloud, I realized that it was a specific description of my own experiences during the two years leading up to that night—details that Bradley couldn't have known unless God had revealed them to him. I knew that message was for me. It was a telegram from God, delivered to me by Bradley Stuart.

Bradley has endured a great deal of suffering, but God is using the pain of his past to mold him into a servant who hears His voice and teaches others to listen. Bradley doesn't dwell on the pain of the past, but chooses instead to press into God—which is why God is now using him in a mighty way.

The Blessing of Thorns

Adversity molded the apostle Paul into the greatest warrior for Christ the world has ever known. But there were times when adversity took its toll on this rugged warrior. We can sense Paul's hurt and discouragement near the end of his second letter to Timothy:

> Do your best to come to me quickly, for Demas, because he loved this world, has deserted me and has gone to Thessalonica. Crescens has gone to Galatia, and Titus to Dalmatia. Only Luke is with me. Get Mark and bring him with you, because he is helpful to me in my ministry. . . . Alexander the metalworker did me a great deal of harm. The Lord will repay him for what he has done. . . . At my first defense, no one came to my support, but everyone deserted me. . . . Do your best to get here before winter (4:9-11,14,16,21).

Do you hear the pain in those words? Twice he urges Timothy to come to him: "Do your best to come to me quickly" and "Do your best to get here before winter." Do you feel his anguish when he twice speaks of being deserted by his friends?

In most of his letters, Paul seems to have an invincible spirit and a hide of steel. Yet he was a man who suffered, felt betrayed, and was sometimes very lonely. However, Paul chose to look at life from a heavenly perspective. That's why he could write:

> We are hard pressed on every side, but not crushed; perplexed, but not in despair; persecuted, but not abandoned; struck down, but not destroyed. We always carry around in our body the death of Jesus, so that the life of Jesus may also be revealed in our body (2 Cor. 4:8-10).

Paul had experienced a level of opposition and suffering that you and I can scarcely imagine. Yet he was not crushed, and he refused to give in to despair. He viewed his life as a continual process of dying. His goal was to live in such a way that the life of Jesus would be revealed in his response to adversity.

Paul also experienced an ongoing burden that he called a "thorn in [his] flesh." Bible scholars have speculated as to what this thorn might have been, but no one knows for sure. We do know that it was so hurtful to Paul that he asked God on three different occasions to remove it from his life:

> To keep me from becoming conceited because of these surpassingly great revelations, there was given me a thorn in my flesh, a messenger of Satan, to torment me. Three times I pleaded with the Lord to take it away from me. But he said to me, "My grace is sufficient for you, for my power is made perfect in weakness." Therefore I will boast all the more gladly about my weaknesses, so that Christ's power may rest on me. That is why, for Christ's sake, I delight in weaknesses, in insults, in hardships, in persecutions, in difficulties. For when I am weak, then I am strong (2 Cor. 12:7-10).

Paul had a great calling on his life. The revelations and faith experiences that God gave him would have been too much for any man's humility. So God, in order to ensure His investment in Paul's life, gave this man a thorn in his flesh to help him maintain a humble, godly perspective.

The bloom of a rose is beautiful, but the thorn of a rose produces only pain. Thorns hurt us and humble us. That is the blessing of thorns.

Dare to Fulfill Your Calling

One day in 1995, I had lunch with Larry Burkett, the president of Christian Financial Concepts (now Crown Ministries). Larry, who passed away in 2003, devoted much of his life to teaching people how to handle money God's way. He wrote more than 70 books, and his radio program was carried on more than 1,000 stations.

At the time I met with Larry, I was in the second year of my Joseph Pit process. Larry and I talked about the trend of new faith-and-work ministry groups emerging throughout the country. He was not aware of the trend but asked if I might bring some of these ministries together for a roundtable discussion.

I agreed to set up a meeting. I sent faxes to leaders of the larger organizations, including Christian Business Men's Committee, Full Gospel Businessmen, and Fellowship of Companies for Christ. Many responded positively. Then I noticed something odd: I began to get requests from organizations I had not contacted—and they all wanted to send representatives. When the event began, 54 people from 45 organizations arrived in Atlanta for a workplace leaders summit. Larry Burkett had planned to come, but cancelled due to a last-minute scheduling conflict. I hosted the meeting myself.

That conference became the birthplace of two distinct ministries. One is Marketplace Leaders (www.marketplaceleaders.org), an equipping ministry designed to help men and women fulfill their calling in their career life. The other is International Coalition of Workplace Ministries (www.icwm.net), an organization designed to cast the vision of the Faith and Work movement by building alliances among workplace believers, workplace ministries, pastors and church leaders. We launched these ministries with vision and enthusiasm, but very little money. During those early years, God provided just enough funding each month to keep them moving forward.

On the flight home from Cyprus in 1998, I sat next to Gunnar Olson. As we talked, he told me candidly, "I've been watching you these past few years and telling the members of my board about you. I said that you reminded me of a brightly colored butterfly, waiting to be born. The adversity you're going through is like the struggle a butterfly goes through as it emerges from a cocoon. What God has been doing in your life is painful, but necessary. I've watched you struggle, and it has taken great discipline on my part to keep from cutting open the cocoon so you could fly out. But I knew that if I did that, you would die. It's the struggle that prepares you to be God's chosen leader."

Gunnar was right. We need the struggle in order to grow strong in our faith. During my struggle, I had quite a few experiences in which God prompted a believer to provide exactly what I needed in that situation—

but no more than I needed. Although my needs for that day or that hour were always met, no one ever came along to break me out of my cocoon and take all of my troubles away. God knew that I needed seven full years of preparation—no more, no less.

Ever since my emergence, God has used me to reach out to people who are going through struggles similar to mine. For example, I recently walked into a local hair salon for a haircut. It was only my second visit to this shop, so the lady with whom I had the appointment was someone I had only met once before.

I entered the shop and said, "Hello, Gail. How are you today?" I was totally unprepared for what happened next. She looked at me, and I could see the intense sadness in her eyes. Then she leaned against me, put her head on my shoulder, and began crying uncontrollably.

"Gail!" I said. "What's wrong?"

For the next few moments, Gail poured out her story. Her marriage was in crisis because her abusive husband was a heavy drug user. As Gail talked, the other customers sat quietly in their chairs. Finally, Gail's tears subsided, and she and I prayed together.

Gail and I talked each time I got my hair cut, but it was months before she could do anything but vent about her husband. Over the next few weeks, I learned more of Gail's story. Although she had attended church for years, she had no walk with God.

In time, Gail began attending a prayer fellowship. Several Christian women became spiritual mentors to her and helped her to build a spiritual foundation through Bible study and prayer. She got out of the abusive marriage, recommitted her life to Jesus Christ, and was baptized.

Gail's life changed dramatically because God sent me to her for a haircut. I walked into her shop at the very moment she could no longer contain her pain and had to talk to someone. It clearly wasn't anything I did, but simply what God in His mercy chose to do through me.

I still go to Gail to get my haircut, and every time I go, I hear story after story of the wonderful things God is doing in her life. She had to go through the Valley of Achor, the Valley of Trouble, to reach the end of herself and seek God with her whole heart. She knows now that God has placed a Joseph Calling on her life. She still works in a hair salon, but she doesn't just cut and style hair. She witnesses to others and claims that hair salon and its clients for the Kingdom.

This is a time of great harvest in God's kingdom. He is sending out His laborers into the office buildings, penthouse suites, banks, stores, shops, industrial parks, factories, foundries, media centers, malls and studios—where people today spend 70 percent of their waking hours. He is shaking up lives and leading His people through the Valley of Achor, where He reshapes their character and transforms their thinking.

Is your Valley of Achor ahead of you? If so, don't fear it—embrace it! God is faithful and He will never leave you.

Are you going through the Valley of Achor right now? God is alongside you. In His perfect timing, your valley will become a doorway to a ministry that you can't even imagine right now.

Have you already been through the Valley of Achor? Are you climbing up the mountain now? Then don't stop. Dare to fulfill your calling. Dare to live the adventure God has planned for you.

Your life up to this moment has been mere preparation for what lies ahead. The road to your destiny is at your feet. The adventure of a lifetime is before you.

God speed you on your journey!

QUESTIONS FOR REFLECTION

1. Morris Ruddick says that a modern-day Joseph is a person who

   ___ hears God's voice and is spiritually in tune with the Lord

   ___ is recognized as one on whom God's favor rests

   ___ speaks the truth boldly, honestly and without fear or equivocation

   ___ has a clear perception of life and operates from God's perspective

   ___ is not limited by manmade tradition, but thinks creatively and innovatively

   ___ understands the times

   ___ is a humble servant-leader

   ___ puts obedience to God's calling ahead of personal wants and desires

   ___ looks to forge strategic alliances in the unlikeliest of places

   ___ spends large amounts of time in the presence of the Lord

   ___ does ministry out in the world's system, not in the religious cloister

   ___ is a mover and shaker in the world of finance, business or government

   Check the qualities that describe you. Next, consider the qualities that you didn't check. Are you asking God to help you build these traits in your life? Do you feel God is working to produce these traits in your life?

2. Consider some test or suffering you went through in the past, especially a trial that seemed meaningless and senseless at the time. Can you think of any way the trial you went through helped change or prepare you in some way? Do you feel you are beginning to gain God's perspective on your trials?

3. Have you ever experienced a paradigm shift in your Christian walk? Describe your old paradigm. Now describe your new paradigm. What caused this transformation in your thinking?

4. Have you been through the Valley of Achor? Are you in the valley now? If you could avoid or escape the Valley of Achor, would you? Should you? Explain your answers.

5. Do you have a thorn in the flesh? Why do you think it won't go away? If Jesus were standing before you right now, what would you say to Him about your thorn?

Note

1. Morris E. Ruddick, *God's Economy, Israel and the Nations* (Longwood, FL: Xulon Press, 2004), p. 18.

Summing It All Up

Just remember . . .

Like Joseph, God calls some leaders to experience extraordinary levels of adversity in order to accomplish extraordinary things through them.

Joseph's dreams had to die before they could come true.

The pathway to leadership almost always takes us through the valley of adversity.

God is more concerned with future potential than present circumstances.

God often takes us through adversity to get our eyes off of our own limitations so that we can see His limitless power.

The greater and higher the calling, the more intense the adversity.

The Judas Test is God's graduate-level course in faith, designed to reveal the truth about ourselves: Are we willing to trust Him enough to forgive the Judases in our lives?

He will not elevate us if there is any root of bitterness in our lives.

Satan will always tempt you in the place of your inheritance.

It's a paradox, but it's true: God often calls us to a ministry and then deliberately thwarts our efforts to achieve our goals!

Sometimes God has to take us into the desert in order to get Egypt out of our system.

God's provision and blessing do not always come at the moment we act in obedience to His calling.

The Judas Test is not about getting the results we want. It's about proving that we trust God enough to forgive our Judases.

It's a mistake to try to rush the work God is doing in our souls.

Perseverance is the key to every great accomplishment because nothing of lasting value has ever been achieved without adversity.

How can you tell when your trial will be over? When it doesn't matter anymore.

Evil, suffering and death came into the world when the first man and woman listened to Satan and committed the first sin.

Obedience can't be viewed as an insurance policy against adversity. Every blessing we receive is a gift of God's grace.

The best way to get beyond our pain is to get outside of ourselves and focus on others.

Sometimes the adversity that comes into our lives is the direct result of sin.

It often takes a crisis to force us to examine ourselves.

God doesn't test us in order to find out something He doesn't already know. He tests us so that we can learn about ourselves and His love, power and faithfulness.

If you hope to succeed, learn everything you can from your failures.

God sees failure as preparation for success.

Our lives are framed by the events and experiences that God takes us through, and our lives are defined by how we respond.

But those who suffer [God] delivers in their suffering; he speaks to them in their affliction" (Job 36:15).

Additional Resources
by Os Hillman

FREE Email Devotional
Start your day by reading an email that encourages you to experience the Lord's presence at work. TGIF Today God Is First is a free daily email subscription which has a scripture verse and brief devotional applied to a workplace situation. Subscribe by going to: www.marketplaceleaders.org

Marketplace Mentor
Twice a month, receive more in-depth Biblical teaching on various topics related to your workplace calling, marketplace tips, proven business principles, and free and discounted resources via this email e-Zine. When you subscribe you'll receive five free ebooks by Os Hillman.

TGIF Today God Is First
365 Meditations on the Principles of Christ in the Workplace.

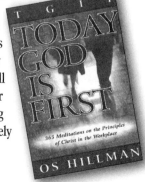

The daily email devotional in book form! Today God Is First provides daily meditations that will help you focus your priority on knowing Jesus more intimately every day.
Hardback, 400 pp.

TGIF Paperback
180 devotionals presented by topics that range from God's will for your life to adversity. The smaller size and weight allows you to carry it with you wherever you go.
Paperback,
286 pp.

TGIF Small Group Bible Study
The popular TGIF Today God Is First book is now a 12-week, small group Bible study that is ideal for workplace groups. This study includes discussion questions; a workplace application with added scriptures that will allow the leader to extend or reduce the study time. Booklet, 48 pp.

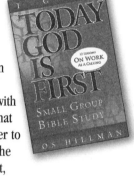

Faith & Work: Do They Mix?
When you have an intimate relationship with Jesus, you will understand that your faith and work are not separate in God's eyes. This book will help you understand why your work IS your ministry.
Paperback,
128 pp.

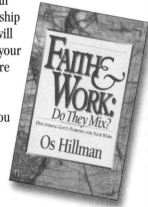

Some products are not available in stores. See one of our websites to order:

www.marketplaceleaders.org or
www.faithandworkresources.com

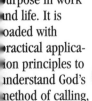
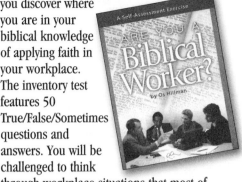
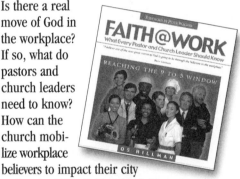

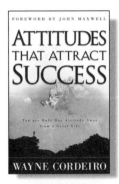
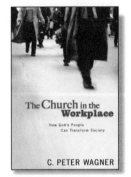

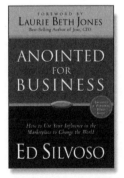